CW00956260

DOMINIC HINDE is a journalist an⟨ He has studied and worked on a for a decade, including writing a University of Edinburgh and a period as a visiting researcher at Sweden's Uppsala University. In his journalistic career Hinde has reported from Scandinavia, Germany, the US, South America and Scotland as a freelance foreign correspondent for *The Scotsman*, *Washington Times*, *USA Today* and others. He has also worked for Danish Public Broadcasting and as a culture columnist for the Swedish news magazine *Flamman*. In addition to journalism, Hinde also translates plays and novels from the Scandinavian languages into English and has taught on Scandinavian culture and politics at both the University of Edinburgh and University College London. *A Utopia Like Any Other* is his first full book.

A Utopia Like Any Other

Inside the Swedish model

DOMINIC HINDE

Luath Press Limited
EDINBURGH
www.luath.co.uk

First published 2016
Reprinted 2016
Reprinted 2017
Reprinted 2020

ISBN: 978-1-910745-32-8

The paper used in this book is recyclable. It is made from
low chlorine pulps produced in a low energy, low emissions manner
from renewable forests.

Printed and bound by
Bell & Bain Ltd., Glasgow

Typeset in 11 point Sabon by
3btype.com

Image 1 sourced from Wikimedia by Self-taken, published under the
terms of the GNU Free Documentation License

Image 10 sourced from Wikimedia and photographed By Jordgubbe

Image 6 sourced from Wikimedia and photographed by Tage Olsin,
own work

Images 15 and 16 photographed by Gigi Chang

Contents

Foreword

IN THE MINDS of anyone on the progressive side of the political spectrum, Scandinavia is always something we talk about in fond terms. Compared with a country like the UK there is much about Scandinavian politics that appears attractive, from the way it organises its democracy to its record on equality and, in the case of Sweden, a pro-active but independent foreign policy. It's natural then that many in Scotland, and especially those of us who don't believe that our future must forever be as part of the UK, see much to draw from as we imagine how we might run our affairs, or our position in the international community.

It is very easy to use Scandinavia as a political tool, and Labour, the Scottish National Party and the Conservatives have all at different times tried to market a supposedly Nordic style of politics. Usually this approach takes advantage of the fact that, though many of us have heard about the social and economic success of the Nordic countries, few are familiar enough to do much other than cherry pick what is presented to us, often only cosmetically. When Scotland regained its Parliament in 1999 there were for example positive noises made about embracing a deliberative, multi-party approach to how we govern. It is fair to say that while a few of these ideas were realised, many were not. When pushed, none of the governing parties in Scotland or the rest of the UK have been prepared to make the shift to that more open style of politics, and although my colleagues and I have sought to introduce fairer, Nordic-inspired tax policies we have generally met with resistance. It's often repeated, and hard to deny, that we cannot have Scandinavian levels of investment in society with American levels of taxation, but political salesmanship has achieved a deferral of the moment when the choice must be made. It can't put it off forever.

Throughout the 20th century the Nordic countries became a model for other European left wing movements to follow, but today we find ourselves in very different circumstances to the postwar years in either the UK or across the North Sea. Few would even try to argue that building the ethnically homogenous society of 20th century Scandinavia was desirable, or even possible. But a movement of normal people pushing for social changes similar to those that forged the Scandinavian welfare states? That seems absolutely within reach.

The challenge now, for politicians in Scandinavia and elsewhere, is to build a more social and more democratic society fit for the future. Perhaps at times we're guilty of too rosy, even utopian, a view of Scandinavia. But a politics of social equity, environmental responsibility and democratic accountability is both a future worth pursuing and absolutely possible.

Patrick Harvie

Introduction

THIS IS A BOOK about Sweden, but also about the changing world at large. It is not supposed to be a political manifesto, but neither is it devoid of politics. The book is a combination of foreign reporting, academic writing and extra material collected along the way, combined to tell a story about the Swedish model, a term familiar to a lot of people without it ever being fully elaborated upon. The period covered by the book was a time of political uncertainty and transition in Sweden, with new pressures and old problems resurfacing as part of the wider upheavals taking place across Europe. This is why this book goes well beyond contemporary Sweden; to suburban Scotland, urban China, and back to the makings of modern Scandinavia and the rise of European Social Democracy in the 1930s.

The idea of producing a book first came about on a train trip from Gothenburg to Stockholm in the September of 2014. It was just after the chaos of Scottish independence referendum and the Swedish general election, a time when seemingly everyone was an expert on the Nordic countries and when 'Swedish-style' was the adjective of choice amongst politicians in Edinburgh looking to sell the independence project to a sometimes sceptical public. Rolling slowly through the small towns of central Sweden, in some ways idyllic but in others deeply troubled, there are many reminders that it is a far more complex country than it is often portrayed as being.

This was rammed home to me in the autumn of 2015 when a translated quote from a newspaper article I had written was lifted without attribution or context; it started popping up all over the internet in click-bait about how Sweden was going to become carbon neutral, the reality of which was more complicated than most of the reporting on it would admit. Similarly, around the same time another piece did the rounds claiming that everyone in Sweden was going to work six hour days – the real story of that particular policy and how it happened is dealt with in the pages of this book – but it was something most readers were perfectly happy to believe and commented on approvingly. Shortly after, I was sat on a panel at a UK book festival where one of the other participants declared 'the values of the Swedish people mean that all their services are publicly owned'. It was both terrifyingly essentialist (the person in question was a relatively prominent left-wing activist) and wholly untrue. It was met with nods of agreement from an audience happy to hear that somewhere there was a place better than where they were.

This phenomenon, the desire to make Sweden whatever people want it to be, is everywhere and is hard to resist. As a freelance correspondent the two most bankable pitches for foreign media are to find something that shows how Sweden is miles ahead of everybody else or to report on the disintegration of a once perfect society. Often when we talk about Sweden abroad we are not interested in the country at all, but in the apparent deficiencies of ourselves and where we happen to live. On numerous occasions I have been told by editors when pitching material from Scandinavia, 'great, but this doesn't really fit with our audience'. Telling a good story and telling the real story are not always the same thing.

In the year in which most of the things that make up this book were written I travelled the country from top to bottom, visiting new places and revisiting old ones. Everywhere you go in Sweden you cannot escape the legacy of the Social Democratic movement that built the country into what it is today; it is pervasive even amongst those who are ideologically opposed to left-wing politics. The people featured within its pages are all real, though some have had their names changed as they did not know they were going to be written about when interviewed. It is in these people's everyday lives that the real politics exists, and where the realities and complexities of Sweden and its much admired model can be found.

Reading the book it will be obvious where I have taken a lot of inspiration from, and I could not have written it without the first class Swedish journalism of both Po Tidholm and Niklas Orrenius as a guide, as well as the welfare work of Irene Wennemo. On a more direct level I have benefited from the help and inside knowledge of a raft of former colleagues in Uppsala. I am grateful to my friend and colleague Gigi Chang for her help in Shanghai, and to Lotte at Luath in Edinburgh for her assistance in putting the book together. I also owe a great amount to the late Helena Forsås Scott, Professor of Swedish and Gender Studies at UCL in London, who sadly passed away during its writing and who made a lasting impression on me and many others.

There is so much about Sweden not mentioned here that deserves coverage, and some things which are best told on the TV or radio instead of on paper. Whatever happens to Sweden in the future, and however it ends up being reported, it is country that it pays to keep an eye on.

Kungliga Biblioteket, Stockholm
August 2015

CHAPTER ONE

Everybody's Utopia

*I think we should look to countries like Denmark,
like Sweden, and Norway and learn from what they
have accomplished for their working people.*
BERNIE SANDERS

IT IS LATE MORNING on a grey Wednesday lunchtime in the
small town of Coatbridge, just to the east of Glasgow in
suburban Scotland. On the high street it looks like any other
day of the week; a few people mill around in the entrance to
the concrete shopping centre as a man sells packs of socks from
a temporary stall under the awning of a closed shop. The only
places doing solid business are the ASDA supermarket and the
turf-green illuminated Celtic FC club store directly opposite.

This is not just a normal Wednesday though. Tomorrow
morning Scotland is due to go to the polls to decide whether
or not it should become an independent country, leaving
Britain for a new life as small Northern European nation.
Coatbridge is typical of the former industrial towns that ring
Scotland's largest city, and until now the closest it has come
to Scandinavia are the replica shirts in the Celtic club store
bearing the name of Sweden striker Henrik Larsson. *Kungen*,
or the King as Larsson was known to his English-speaking
fans, is a legend in Glasgow's eastern suburbs. Part of Celtic
mythology, he did Sweden's reputation no damage during his
Scottish stay before taking his considerable talents on to
Barcelona and Manchester United.

In Larsson's footsteps comes a Scandinavian film crew,
trying to find out what Scottish people think not only about

independence, but also their potential new place in a reorganised continent alongside their Scandinavian neighbours. The region has loomed large in the campaign, with meeting rooms around the country filled with talk of Nordic prosperity and new northern horizons for the North Atlantic country. In response, members of the anti-independence campaign appeared on television with scare stories of 80 per cent tax rates and dystopian state controls, arguing with pro-independence voices that talked of political cooperation, Nordic peacekeeping and a cultural revival that would make Scotland as chic as the rest of the North Atlantic.

In a high concrete tower block overlooking Coatbridge town centre the TV crew knock on doors looking for interviewees. People are either not home or not interested. Eventually though they find someone prepared to talk to them, a former taxi-driver turned council cleaner mopping the lino-furnished landings between floors, ten stories up in the granite grey of the Scottish morning. The TV anchor, an experienced half Swedish, half Danish woman used to trawling Europe for stories, jumps in with her initial question after some encouragement.

'Hi there, we're filming for a Nordic television programme about the referendum and wondered if you wanted to talk about how you will vote tomorrow,' she says with a persistent friendliness. The interviewee looks up from his mop. After some pushing he finally agrees to be filmed, and the arrival of two Swedish speaking crew gives him further encouragement.

'I think I'll vote Yes,' he says with some consideration. 'People are talking about it being more equal, more like Norway and Sweden and those countries.'

The reporter nods away, indicating he should say more.

'It would be for the kids. You've got a pretty good impression of how they do things, and if Scotland could be more like that then it seems a good chance.' Like many voters in Scotland, he has been reached by the ubiquitous pro-independence narrative of a nation reborn as a leading light of Northern Europe. The governing Scottish National Party have been talking about a North Atlantic 'arc of prosperity' and civic groups have been eagerly importing speakers from all over Northern Europe to talk about the country's potential path, packing community meetings and articulating a different country from the one most Scots live in. The details however are sketchy, and the motivations range from environmental awareness and education to gender equality and economic success. Whatever the substance, the effect is unambiguous – Scandinavia is there to be copied and admired.

Brand Scandinavia has a worldwide reach far beyond Scotland's central belt though, from members of the European left wanting to build their own social democracies to the Chinese middle class paying for mass produced designer furniture at IKEA stores in Beijing, or American TV executives snapping up the rights to Nordic drama. In Scotland's case brand Scandinavia means reinventing the country as a better version of itself along the lines of an imagined north. It is a composite vision in which Scotland could have Danish wind and Norwegian oil, Icelandic fishing and Swedish industry. For many voters in Scotland's independence referendum their Scandinavian neighbours offered a glimpse of a more radical, less granite-grey future. In the same vein, England has been sold Swedish free schools, France has embraced *le modèle suédois* in its sex work policy and Democratic presidential hopeful Bernie Sanders has singled out Sweden and its neighbours as a blueprint for a new America. Neither is this love of the Nordic a new phenomenon. The Nordic countries, and Sweden in particular, have always attracted a special kind of attention from utopian dreamers. In 1796

Mary Wollstonecraft, the English feminist and political philosopher, wrote a travel diary based on her time in Scandinavia in which the region was used as a canvas for what a radical and more egalitarian Britain might look like. The book sold well and unleashed a small wave of idealistic Nordic romanticism in the people around Wollstonecraft, exploiting the fact that few had first-hand experience of the places she visited

More than a century later, a then largely unknown American journalist called Marquis Childs pitched up in Stockholm. His stay would result in a work that came to shape many people's views of what internationally became known as the Swedish Model. *Sweden: The Middle Way* was a bestseller in the English-speaking world upon its publication, portraying a harmonious society in which big business had been made to bow to the will of the people and enlightened Social Democratic government had led the country on a pragmatic path between the twin perils of Anglo-Saxon capitalism and European totalitarianism. Including audiences with senior politicians and the working man, *The Middle Way* offered a glowing appraisal of Sweden's path from poverty to cohesive market socialism that was the polar opposite of the depression-scarred '30s United States Childs had left behind.

Childs' Sweden was populated by altruistic planners and modest politicians working for a common good in well-designed houses and bright factories. Touring cooperative flour mills and interviewing the Prime Minister, his trip through a picturebook Sweden which combined cosy tradition with clean, modern market socialism left its mark on the British and American public. Eighty years on the narrative is remarkably similar, even if the world around has changed beyond all recognition.

Despite his enthusiasm for Sweden's political project Childs was not an economist and never set out to write about Sweden's burgeoning social democracy. He had originally travelled to Stockholm to attend a housing expo but returned having discovered what seemed to be a perfect society in the making. In the cultural essentialism of the pre-war years he was able to describe Swedes as a model race imbued with 'certain basic characteristics – patience, intelligence, perseverance, courage', and a democracy which 'sprang from something inherent in the nature of the people.' At the same time as the Swedish model was painted as an example for others to follow, Swedes were granted an exceptional position in an idealised pastoral socialism straight from the pages of a propaganda pamphlet.

The expo that Childs set out to cover was also anything but typical of the country it was in. Staged with considerable effort on the part of its organisers, the Stockholm Exhibition of 1930 was intended as an exercise in aspiration and utopian modernism that had yet to reach out beyond Sweden's cities. Allan Pred, an American geographer who became one of the most nuanced commentators of Sweden's global image, summarised the entire Stockholm Exhibition as nothing less than an elaborate attempt to market Sweden abroad.

Different pavilions at the exhibition documented Swedish achievements and Swedish Ambitions in technology and the arts. One of the main drivers behind the entire project was Gunnar Asplund, who was to become synonymous with the clean and bright image of modern Sweden. In fact at the centre of the Stockholm exhibition was an Asplund-designed restaurant with the word Paradiset – Swedish for paradise – emblazoned on its front. As long as the temporary exhibition lasted it offered a glimpse of Swedish utopia made real, with politics meeting design and culture in an alluring crystalline vision of a forward-looking, clean, and altogether better world.

Three decades later, another journalist landed in Stockholm to find out about the modern Swedish miracle that Childs had uncovered. David Frost is better known to the wider world as the man who would engineer an interview with the disgraced Richard Nixon after the Watergate scandal, but in 1969 he conducted a seminal televised interrogation of a young and intellectually sharp Swedish politician, in search of answers about the country's model society. The man in the chair opposite Frost was Olof Palme, Sweden's Social Democratic Education Minister and Prime Minister in waiting. As head of government he would help to cement Sweden's political reputation internationally through his defence of the Swedish model from the pressures of American economic imperialism and Soviet expansionism alike. A consummate statesman, Palme has since become faded, a symbol of the golden years of Sweden's social democratic settlement. In the minimal surroundings of a Stockholm TV studio and seated on two leather armchairs designed by Le Corbusier, Frost probed Palme about the Swedish way. In the days beforehand the domestic press had promised an epic battle between the two heavyweights, but the visiting interviewer was met by a disarmingly cool and assured opponent. Frost's challenging and provocative style demanded that Palme represent not just himself but the entire Swedish nation, from foreign policy to social reform. Defending opposition to the Vietnam War and being coy about his leadership ambitions, Palme calmly attacked the Anglo-Saxon political model and threw Frost's questions back at him.

'If you could look at one place and say "David, that's the real Sweden," where would you tell me to look?' began Frost in his trademark laid-back style.

'I can't,' came the politician's reply. 'To a foreigner this is might seem a small and dull country, but to me it is a country with infinite variety... there is not any one particular place that is Sweden.' Unhappy with the answer, Frost probed again, 'What is the essence of being Swedish?'

'We are often pictured as a country that has solved its problems,' replied Palme after some consideration. 'There are a great amount of unsolved problems in this country, and to solve these problems we need a sense of community.' Palme's answer revealed one of the core characteristics of the Swedish model – the nation state as political project. The community that Palme hinted at was the People's Home, or *folkhem*, an understanding of the interdependence of people within the country where the nation was seen as a single family. A political undertaking synonymous with a nationality, it had been introduced by former Prime Minister Per Albin Hansson, a man Marquis Childs had encountered on his visit to 1930s Stockholm. As Gunnar Asplund and his architectural contemporaries tried to build homes for people, the Swedish Social Democratic Party tried to build a single home for everyone in which all could flourish.

Despite his claims to represent the working man, Palme was as typical of the average Swede as Asplund's pavilion marked 'paradise' was of the everyday lives of most people. Born into an aristocratic family and able to travel widely, he was an intellectual rather than a union man with a moral gravitas that won him plaudits around the world. Raised in the wealthy Östermalm district of Stockholm and educated at elite schools in Sweden and the US, his polished English tones mirrored his similarly refined Swedish. With his abandonment of privilege and his modest family house in Stockholm's western suburbs, he embodied a vision of a new classless society. It was a vision he took with him around the world.

Where Wollstonecraft, Childs and Frost led many have followed. The idea of a golden middle way to be copied has become rhetorical currency amongst the European left and even some Liberals and Conservatives. The British sociologist Anthony Giddens used the concept extensively to describe a new kind of social democratic society, and it was in turn used by Tony Blair and Bill Clinton in their own political projects of the 1990s to promote an inclusive and cohesive vision of a society where all could succeed and thrive.

Neither is this admiration without foundation; from the 1960s to the 1980s Sweden had the lowest levels of inequality in the developed world by a considerable degree. When the celebrity French economist Thomas Piketty released his bestselling critique of global inequality, *Capital in the 21st Century*, he used the country as a case study, showing how Sweden had succeeded where others seemed to have failed.[1] Piketty compared it to France, Britain and the US as an example of how different countries had evolved and managed their economies, with Sweden going further than any other developed country in reducing the huge disparities between wealth and poverty that existed in Europe at the beginning of the 20th century during the Belle Époque.

Together with its longstanding reputation for economic egalitarianism, in time the Swedish model developed to encompass gender equality and environmental responsibility on the global stage. Sweden itself meanwhile has wholeheartedly embraced the view that it is something special. This fusion, or confusion, of culture and politics is produced and reproduced worldwide across the media, from internet listicles on modern Swedish fathers to bestselling recipe books and conventions for fans of Swedish culture. In many cases the country is reduced to a lifestyle choice with vague connotations towards what the people buying it want to believe in and what Sweden itself wants people to believe.

1 See graph on page 62.

The statistics though speak for themselves. Sweden is ranked fourth in the world for gender equality by the World Economic Forum and has been declared the world's most sustainable country by one green investment monitor, also holding a high place in the Yale University global environmental performance rankings. It also regularly features in the top-ten on the Human Development Index, a UN-backed ranking of countries which collates wealth, education, opportunity and life expectancy. This creates a complex picture in which Sweden is often presented as a vision of future society devoid of the problems which beset the rest of the world, or by its detractors as something far more sinister. Yet somewhere behind these international rankings, national branding campaigns and the utopian dreaming exists a real country occupied by real people; safe and clean and green and modern. Where, in the words of David Frost, is the real Sweden, and where is the line between utopian fiction and reality? What is the Swedish model, who are the people who live in it, and moreover, what is it good for?

CHAPTER TWO

A Workers' Utopia

How Sweden made work pay

Our task is to make clear to workers that even in the
apparently equal society of today, a class struggle is
underway.

HJALMAR BRANTING

THE UPPER-CLASS suburb of Saltsjöbaden, just outside
Stockholm, is not an obvious site of socialist pilgrimage.
With its marina, health clinics and wide vista onto the
Stockholm archipelago, the bathing resort is a storybook
Nordic town peopled with wealthy old women walking
small dogs and urbanites who have made good in the city. It
was, however, the scene of perhaps the most important event
in the making of the Swedish model of employment.

To get there visitors must ride a clattering railway recycled
from the cast-offs of the Stockholm metro system. It jolts along
through the trees of the Stockholm archipelago, stopping at
wooden stations next to a row of boats neatly lined up along
the shore. At each stop teenagers with slicked back hair and
iPhones get on and off, the girls with luxury Michael Kors
handbags and the boys in high-end branded puffer jackets.

Despite the trappings of luxury, Saltsjöbaden was the
location of a meeting that came to define the Swedish model.
In the centre of the resort, and towering over it, is the wedding-
cake Grand Hotel, icing white with turrets and balconies
looming above the promenade. It was here, in 1938, that the
Swedish Council of Trade Unions and the Swedish Employer's

Association sat down and signed the Saltsjöbad agreement, whereby both sides pledged to enter into a system of collective bargaining. The collective agreements dictate how much people earn and what rights they can expect, and the basics of it are still in force almost 80 years on.

On a Monday morning in February the snow has turned to ice on the Grand Hotel's long drive and the last few guests on Valentine's weekend deals are checking out at the polished wood reception which looks out onto the bobbing boats in the harbour. The hotel's empty corridors are manned by fewer staff than were intended for them, and one of the two people at the front desk is periodically forced to leave in order to attend to guests. The balconies are empty despite the bright winter sun and the veranda is still covered in snow. The bell-boys and attendants are long gone; the only remaining hint of luxury is a wealthy Russian couple struggling to open one of the doors from the veranda as a Ludovico Einaudi CD loops piano music across the imitation log fire in the grate.

In the base of one of the building's ostentatious turrets, in a tiny office, sits the Grand Hotel's finance officer. A middle aged woman surrounded by pictures of dogs and lever-arch files containing pay slips and invoices, she is the hotel's longest serving employee. The collective agreements that underpin the Swedish economy mean that nobody on her spreadsheet will earn less than around 120 kronor an hour, with many earning much more. This is almost double the minimum wage of the US and a third higher than in Britain.

'Most people are members,' she says matter of factly. The hotel has signed the collective deal with the union, meaning it has to both pay the minimum wage and provide requisite holiday time. All Swedes are entitled to a minimum of five weeks holiday, but many unions have been successful in winning more for their members. Other perks include paid time off to go to the gym and flexible hours to help with childcare. The couples checking in for long Valentine's weekends in the faded glamour of the Grand Hotel are making good use of it.

'The hotel follows the rules, and we get together once a year to discuss conditions and any changes,' says the finance officer. As to whether it works, she is fairly positive, though the hotel manager standing in the corner may have something to do with it. 'It does not really limit flexibility,' she claims.

It seems like an agreeable arrangement, but contrary to the cosy view of the Swedish system often portrayed abroad, the collective bargaining approach was invented as an answer to a series of strikes and sanctions by both workers and employers which had led to an impasse. It was difficult for either unions or employers to trust one another, and the consensual attitude to negotiations presented in tandem with the Swedish model came as the result of almost 40 years of destructive conflict. This inherently destructive cycle – and the uncertainty it bought to both businesses and workers – meant that non-strike agreements became more common. To the Anglo-Saxon labour model, agreeing not to take industrial action seems counterproductive, but the Swedish system used the threat of industrial unrest to engineer long term respect between the parties. Withholding their labour was only ruled out by workers for as long as employers kept their own end of the bargain.

The roots of the system ratified at Saltsjöbaden stretch back to 1885, when stonemasons in Stockholm organised against an open market on labour and a movement began to grow. In 1905 an agreement was signed that for the first time fixing conditions within a specific sector, the manufacturing industry. The following year employers recognised the right of workers to form unions, but the trade-off was letting employers decide on and lead the work, a hard sell to some of the more radical trade unionists of the period gunning for class revolution. Levels of inequality in Sweden were still high, and even as much of the rest of Europe plotted revolution there was disagreement about the course of action the Swedish working class should take.

Despite its early successes, until 1928 there was no official recognition of the agreed upon system. This meant that if an employer chose to ignore deals with specific unions then strikes would not be far behind. Well into the 1930s millions of hours a year were lost in industrial disputes, and the 1938 meeting of employers and unions in Saltsjöbaden was not an altruistic undertaking from either side. The simmering tensions in the labour market came to a head in 1931 when the army gunned down striking workers at a sawmill in Ådalen in the north of the country. It provoked nationwide outrage and almost split the union movement, a bloody fleck on the time-line of Sweden's long revolution.

It was a revolution that laid the foundations for a particular type of social democratic society that did not require government intervention to keep it going. Although the Social Democrats were Sweden's biggest party for all of the 20th century's latter half, it was the trade unions who helped deliver the working conditions and advances in wages that have made Sweden one of the most desirable countries in the world in which to live and work. Even in the 1960s when Social Democracy was at its peak, Britain had more nationalised companies than Sweden. In Sweden the government tended to take a back seat, embedding the bargaining processes of unions and employers in law but not telling either negotiating party what they should do. Unlike Britain, where the trade union movement is linked heavily to the Labour Party and directly finances it, Sweden's Trade Union Confederation has been crucial to the development of the Swedish economy relatively independent of the Social Democrats.

The knock-on effect of this hands-off approach to labour was that trade unions and the business lobby were soon given representation on the boards of key organisations including labour courts and public companies. This means that Sweden has a relatively weak state apparatus, to the extent it is reliant on the cooperation of such large non-state organisations in its economic framework, but also in its politics. The headquarters of the Swedish Council of Trade Unions, LO, is known as the LO castle. Situated just north of Stockholm's central station, it physically resembles a fortress with its two round towers and palatial entrance, standing as an iconic symbol of the power of the union movement in the public consciousness.

Sweden's delicate triangle of government, business and unions led to the development of a corporate state which tried to manage capitalism, and as long as wages kept rising and Swedish industry expanded the system functioned relatively well. This ability to adapt to markets meant that the government let unprofitable companies go to the wall. In the darkest days of de-industrialisation in the Swedish north it was a running joke that the employment service, AMS, was shorthand for 'all must go south'. Swedish Social Democracy did not so much try to fight capitalism as appropriate it from its masters.

The collective agreements also mean that, when subject to one, employing non-unionised labour on worse terms than the agreement breaks that agreement, even when nobody from the unionised workforce is directly affected. Like its Nordic neighbours Sweden has no minimum wage, instead relying on unions and employers to keep earnings and working conditions in tempo with the needs of the workforce and the changing state of the economy.

According to the conventional narratives of contemporary global economics, such an addiction to high wages should make Sweden a financial disaster. Its labour should have been undercut elsewhere and its businesses should have folded due to the high costs of employment, its workforce overpaid and unproductive. The fact that it has not has depended to a high degree on the thinking of two men; since the Second World War Sweden has generally followed what is known as the Rehn-Meidner model, invented by the social democratic economists Gösta Rehn and Rudolf Meidner in the late 1940s. Under Rehn-Meidner the economy was encouraged to grow exponentially on the understanding that this would subsequently lead to higher tax takings and further investments in welfare and public services as part of a positive spiral. This would further serve to increase consumer demand for goods and services in tandem with a robust union movement which constantly pushed for better wages and conditions on the back of the explosive economic growth. Riding on the coat-tails of modernity and technological advancement, it was the postwar Western European settlement in overdrive.

A few stops into the city from Saltsjöbaden's wooden platform stands Nacka Forum, a sprawling shopping complex catering to the wealthy south-eastern suburbs of Stockholm. On a Sunday afternoon people mill about here with children in tow, eating sushi and drinking smoothies. The names of the stores are half-familiar Swedish approximations of American titles that do not exist across the Atlantic. Wayne's Coffee, Taco Bar and Marks N Brands are all idiosyncratically Swedish articulations of American consumerism. Also present is the Swedish giant at home in any shopping mall worldwide, H&M.

Sprawling malls like Nacka Forum are where Sweden's middle class can come to spend their high wages, and modern

Stockholm is a city in which retail has been made easy. The car park here has spaces for 1900 cars and the people behind those cars' steering wheels have money. Earlier this year a leading Swedish design business chose to open its first physical store at Nacka Forum – the press release boasted that 'Nacka Forum's customers are extremely trend and design conscious.' Put more bluntly, they consume, and it keeps the economy ticking over in a way that Gösta Rehn and Rudolf Meidner would likely approve of.

The collective bargaining systems agreed at Saltsjöbaden were key to the Rehn Meidner model working, guaranteeing that the fruits of capital landed in the pockets of the people and kept the economy turning. In the mid-1980s, as Sweden topped equality measures, the total revenues of Sweden's 50 largest companies exceeded total Swedish GDP, due mostly to their overseas investments. It was, paradoxically, a rare example of capitalist trickle-down economics working in practice.

The Wallenberg dynasty who built Saltsjöbaden's Grand Hotel were at one point estimated to have owned around a third of Sweden's total wealth assets through shareholdings. This included signature giants of Swedish industry such as Electrolux, Saab, Ericsson electronics and the pharmaceutical giant AstraZeneca. The success of Swedish capitalism abroad was integral to the development of socialism at home.

Only once has this model of private enterprise and public benefit been seriously challenged – in the 1980s Sweden experimented with *löntagarfonder*, a system where the profits of private companies were channeled into employee funds which would then allow employees to purchase shares in companies using 'surplus profit'. The brainchild of Rudolf Meidner among others, it was designed to deal with the tendency in the Swedish model for high performing companies to generate profits above and beyond increases in wages that meant those with assets and other shareholdings still raced ahead. In many areas the amount earned by employees did not increase at the same rate as the assets and output of the companies they worked for, and the solution suggested by Meidner and the trade unions was to give employees a share in the ownership of such organisations. For many though it was a step too far, and the policy was abolished in the early 1990s by a one-term right-wing government, never to return.

At the start of 2015 the business and labour ends of the Swedish model met in spectacular fashion. The low-cost airline Norwegian, which had built a phenomenal business on providing cheap flights for well-remunerated Scandinavians to Dubai, New York and Thailand alongside more prosaic and colder destinations, attempted to streamline its business.

As part of this restructuring it attempted to transfer its Swedish and Norwegian pilots to new arms-length companies from which it could then hire them back. A common practice in the tax-efficient aviation industry, this would have meant that the company itself was no longer the direct employer, and as such it would not be liable for the losses that might be incurred. Norwegian already operated a Dublin-registered transatlantic arm that allowed it to take advantage of the rock bottom tax levels successive Irish governments have adopted. Norwegian's chairman Bjørn Kjos was a golden boy of Scandinavian entrepreneurial capitalism, feted for leading rapid expansion in one of the Nordic countries' business success stories. With each new edition of the Norwegian in-flight catalogue the chairman would boast about how rapidly the company was growing, Norwegian was supposed to be a shining example of Scandinavian entrepreneurship, plastering the tail fins of its aircraft with famous Nordic writers, explorers and sportspeople.

The problem for Norwegian was that taking the pilots out and reemploying them would have removed them from collective bargaining agreements in both Norway and Sweden. The pilots dug in, Norwegian's shares tumbled and a newspaper revealed that Kjos had personally dumped over three million pounds worth of company stock on the Oslo stock exchange. The head of the pilots' union compared the company's tactics to being asked to negotiate 'with a gun to the head'. It was a far cry from the third-way utopia of business and labour working in unison which characterised the staff profiles in the company magazine.

Across Norway, Sweden and Denmark, Norwegian's aircraft sat in neat rows on the ground in the weak spring sunshine. Day after day flights were cancelled as their main rivals, SAS, a firm who Norwegian had made capital out of competing with and with whom there was no love lost, carried on as normal. It was estimated that Norwegian lost almost 50 million pounds in revenue as they flew too close to the sun, and eventually they were forced to yield. The collective agreements stayed.

To make matters worse for Kjos, he was booked onto the pan-Scandinavian chat show *Skavlan* to try and repair the damage caused by the strike. Unfortunately the fallen star had the bad luck to be sharing the sofa with none other than Thomas Piketty, invited on to talk about how capital accumulation was increasing global inequality and how a tax on the assets of the wealthy was a potential solution.

'My pilots earn more than I do,' complained the Norwegian director as he railed against the power of the unions.

'Yes, but how much are you worth?' asked Piketty.

'Not as much as I was before the strike.' came the nervous reply from the airline magnate.

Despite the efforts of the pilots' union, the flights to New

York and the Far East kept on rolling, using foreign crew without the luxury of such generous labour protection. In the station café in Saltsjöbaden, couples with pushchairs chat about their latest winter-sun breaks to Thailand.

'It was wonderful, just like a Swedish summer day,' says one woman. Every day several flights depart Stockholm's Arlanda airport for Sweden's paradise colonies in the Far East, where Swedish wages go a long way and the luxury hotel rooms costs a fraction of those available behind the crumbling plaster walls of the Grand Hotel. The high pay packets enjoyed by most Swedes mean that they are a global upper middle class with a purchasing power above and beyond even the average European.

This global disparity was illustrated perfectly in an election poster produced by the conservative Moderate party at the 2014 election. The poster showed a happy blonde nuclear family standing on a Thai beach under a burning sunset. Its text warned that a vote for the Green party would mean a few hundred pounds more on a Thai holiday thanks to aviation levies. Saltsjöbaden is a fortress for the Moderates and the other right-wing parties as formidable as the LO castle.

Despite the prosperity it has brought to working Swedes, the role of the trade unions in keeping wages up is not universally appreciated. In 2010 the youth wing of the Centre Party unveiled what in hindsight proved to be a poorly worded campaign titled 'Fuck Facket Forever', a broadside straight at the wall of the LO castle. *Facket* is shorthand for the Swedish union movement, and under the justification that 'the labour market is a joke and we want to breathe some life into politics' the Centre's youth politicians painted a picture of the trade unions as a behemoth that restricted people's ability to work on their own terms.

This ill-judged attempt to liberate young people from the

chains of the collective agreements was not unique though. The vocabulary of contemporary Sweden is one of entrepreneurship, personal success and achieving your dreams, with little room for pausing to think of others Visible on the posters of the metro system and the lifestyle ads of metropolitan Stockholm, it runs counter to the traditional view of the country as having a subconsciously reinforced egalitarianism. Entrepreneurialism has become a byword for success, and self-sacrifice is part of the road to achieving personal dreams. If success is forthcoming a house in Saltjöbaden or one of Stockholm's other wealthy suburbs awaits.

In 2013 the politically blue town was the site of a spectacular train crash that shattered the suburban silence. One of the aging motor coaches of the little blue commuter train ran away after a cleaner accidentally released the brakes in the early hours of the morning. It plowed through the buffers, and into a block of luxury waterside apartments on the other side. The young woman who had inadvertently taken the controls was seriously injured, and as she lay unconscious in an intensive care unit her employers accused her of having stolen the train. She came away with serious chest and leg injuries, and it was subsequently proven that the private franchisee Arriva had not taken the correct safety measures. Her union subsequently sued Arriva and won.

When the runaway train careered into the house, it was an audible and tangible reminder to the well-heeled of Saltsjöbaden that Sweden still has a working class beyond its clean and rich suburbia, even if they are not always visible. Sweden's unseen workforce operate after hours, cleaning its metro trains and offices, washing dishes and stacking shelves At present divisions in income between the top and bottom of Swedish society are increasing because professional wages have outstripped basic wages as the economy has grown, and this shows no sign of abating. It is part of a worldwide trend, and one that even Sweden's generous pay packets seem unable to reverse. Many lower earning jobs are carried out by women too, keeping the gender pay gap firmly in place.

A year on from the crash, and the luxury apartments that felt the full force of the speeding train have been repaired, though the Grand Hotel is looking slightly worse for wear. The paint may be flaking and the plants may have plastic drip trays, but the hotel's greatest legacy is borne out across the country in the pay of its blue collar professions. An elderly couple walking past with their dog summarise its fate.

'No, not really a luxury hotel any more, it is all people on conferences and spa weekends now. I think it was bought up by an Arab', they say.

The Wallenberg family divested themselves of the Grand Hotel a few years ago for more profitable assets – now it is owned by a Danish-Egyptian hotel magnate. In Stockholm meanwhile, the old rallying cries of the workers have been resurrected. As the little blue train to Saltsjöbaden rumbles into the city centre it passes a billboard with the words *Alla ska med* six foot high, an old Social Democratic slogan meaning 'everyone all together' on a metaphorical journey to a better future. Today it is being used to advertise five-door-Minis big enough for a family. The new Swedish model comes in a range of colours rather than just red. On a poster at the end of the carriage, a trade union advert reminds people that even the self-employed can join up. A young, laughing female businesswoman illustrates the point. In the age of the entrepreneur, there's more of a reason than ever to stick together.

CHAPTER THREE

Democratic Utopia

Sweden's diverse democracy

Land skall med lag byggas – with law the land shall be built
KING KARL XV

IT IS 1:55PM in the Swedish parliament and a buzzer rings to call members to the main chamber. The soft blue stools of the parliamentary deputies are arranged in a wide semicircle that slopes gently upwards toward the back of the room. On the back wall hangs a huge tapestry, entitled *Memories of a Landscape*, symbolically made up of fabric from different parts of the country.

In its shadow stand politicians from all parts of the Swedish nation, all with different accents and each wearing the badges of one of the eight parties represented in the national parliament, the *Riksdag*. At the front of the room sit members of the cabinet on a row of chairs, ready to answer questions from the floor. Today the big hitters among them are the Green Education Minister Gustav Fridolin and the Foreign Minister Margot Wallström, a Social Democrat. The Prime Minister appears once a month, but the way Swedish government is run means they are less important to the working of the parliament. Instead ministers take it in turns to answer questions relevant to their portfolios and party responsibilities.

At first glance the lineup of Government ministers at the front of the room is a dream-team for marketing progressive

Sweden. Education Minister Fridolin is barely in his thirties, a wholesome and media savvy young man who joined the Green Party at just 11 years old. Seated next to him, Wallström is a former EU Environment Commissioner and UN special representative on violence against women. Her signature policy is the development of a self-proclaimed feminist foreign policy, run jointly with the Greens' international development secretary. The Foreign Minister is a far more recognisable face on the international circuit than the less polished and everyday Prime Minister Stefan Löfven. Unfortunately for Wallström and Fridolin's noble ambitions, realpolitik means that an arms treaty on the table with Saudi Arabia makes for some uncomfortable questions from the floor. Arms manufacture makes Sweden a lot of money, and whether it is fighter jets or machine guns on the table, their existence means even the most moral of politicians must consider the economic implications of cutting off such a profitable income stream. Löfven and several other senior Social Democrats have connections to trade unions for whom arms jobs are important, and there have been internal disagreements behind the scenes in the run up to the afternoon's questions. Whatever the questions posed from the floor, there is an even more troubling spectre haunting the idyllic scene of a progressive government on the up, and he is sat directly behind the cabinet.

The 2014 elections in Sweden saw an unprecedented result for the far-right Sweden Democrats party. Beating Fridolin's Greens into fourth place by some margin, the party won themselves one of the deputy speaker positions in the *Riksdag*, and today the countdown clock is controlled by Björn Söder, a shaven-headed Sweden Democrat in a sports jacket.

Söder barely utters a word throughout the one hour session beyond a stern *tack* to remind the speakers that their time is up. His eyes, though, speak volumes as members of the various parties make demands to the ministers, including the gaggle of his own MPs grouped defensively halfway back in the near empty hall. One of the questions makes Söder sit particularly uncomfortably in his seat. Amineh Kakabaveh is an Iranian-born, ethnically Kurdish member of the Swedish Left party. Alone at the back of the chamber, she stands up with a clearly audible foreign accent to her Swedish. Her question is about how the government can help to rebuild Kobane, the city in Syria ravaged by forces of the Islamic State tearing through the Middle East.

The left are the existential enemies of the Sweden Democrats, the single point on which they agree. In an earlier session to swear in the new parliamentarians, one of Kakabaveh's party colleagues publicly told Söder 'you are not my speaker'. When the news of the Sweden Democrat's huge gains reached the Left Party on election night cries of 'No racists on our streets' rung out across the room. There is no love lost between the left and right extremities of the chamber.

Today though Söder is not the one talking, and Margot Wallström answers Kakabaveh's question in the allotted time. Other issues on the table range from nuclear decommissioning to the provision of childcare for foreign researchers at Swedish universities. It is in these empty weekday afternoons that the mundane business of parliament goes on. Eventually the hour is up and Söder leaves without any pleasantries exchanged, officially accepted but privately ostracised.

Outside the chamber Fridolin is met by a small crowd of journalists, including a reporter from the tabloid paper *Expressen* who has spent an hour sitting bored-faced in the press room to get her quote. The Education Minister walks and talks along the wide arc of the wooden-paneled corridor behind the *Riksdag* chamber like a consummate politician.

His red-green coalition lacks a full majority and only just survived an attempt by Söder and his fellow Sweden Democrats to topple it, but the assured smile on which he has built his political career remains.

'After eight years of right wing government there are a range of challenges to tackle, in schools, the environment and in questions of global justice,' he says in a well-rehearsed pitch. 'It is great that Sweden has joined what I soon believe will be a majority of governments in Europe which either have or have had a Green party in a position of power.'

His confidence belies the difficult situation he finds himself in as he waves and moves off again. Some people in Sweden do not finish university until they are 30. Fridolin however has managed to find the time to become a government minister and pursue separate careers as a teacher and TV journalist in between. He vanishes to leave an empty corridor filled only with press teams packing up cameras and a cluster of G4S branded security guards on the lookout for trouble that will never come.

The *Riksdag* building has the air of a more upmarket version of the cruise ships that dock at the quay further down Stockholm's waterfront. Sat on its own island between the rapids at the meeting of freshwater and saltwater in the very centre of the capital, its corridors have the feeling of sweeping panoramic decks linked by escalators. The only thing missing from the auditorium of the main chamber is a bar, and in the foyer is a post office and travel agent to keep politicians in touch with their far flung electoral districts.

In the café one floor down from the chamber Magda Rasmusson and Hanna Wagenius wave to members of their respective parties sat at the tables, each finished with a small square doily and a candle like countless municipal buildings across Sweden. Rasmusson and Wagenius are the youth leaders of the Green and Centre parties, quite at home amongst the senior politicians milling about. Both in their 20s, they sit on different sides of the dividing line, or *blockgräns*, that has traditionally run down the middle of Swedish politics. In the one camp sit the Greens, Social Democrats and the Left Party and in the other the Christian Democrats, conservative Moderates, Liberal and Centre parties occupy a so-called 'bourgeois' bloc. On their own on the far right is the solitary but swelling group of Sweden Democrats.

Despite their economic preferences, the two young politicians have a great deal in common. Both are avowed feminists and both are keen to protect the environment. Irrespective of left or right, they share a certain generational politics that transcends the traditional markers of political allegiance. Wagenius is from Härjedalen, Sweden's smallest municipality by population. The country does not get much more rural, and this was the Centre's historic strength. Born out of an agrarian cooperative liberalism, the Centre once led governments and were the foremost campaigners for the environment in the radical days of the '60s and '70s. They also contributed towards building the Swedish welfare state from a rural standpoint, working to improve conditions for rural labour. Now though, they have a more sympathetic view of nuclear power, unrestrained capitalism and motorway building than their forefathers exhibited, with Rasmusson's party keen to assume the mantle of progressive environmentalism in their place.

Rasmusson is a Stockholmer, and the Greens are a young largely urban party born out of a dissatisfaction with institutional politics and the one size fits all leftism of the two red parties. The only party with a radical vision for the future to their fans and a hopelessly middle class pressure group to their detractors, they are still learning to negotiate the quickly changing maze of Swedish democracy. A local councillor and reserve parliamentary deputy, Rasmusson is hotly tipped for great things. For now though, she and Wagenius are concentrating on reaching out to young people.

'The point of youth politics is that it should work as a democracy school,' says Wagenius. The generous state funding for Sweden's youth politics pays for offices and salaries, discussion weekends, seminars and educational courses. Now more than ever Sweden has had to practice democracy for better or worse. The complex maths of the new Swedish political settlement means bridge building, negotiations and compromises. In 2014 the government survived by the skin of its teeth after agreeing a cross-party consensus to reduce the influence of the far right.

'Opposition is important too', says Rasmusson. 'I wouldn't want to see a unity government with only one party locked out. You need clear lines between the parties, but also to be able to have a dialogue there.' The multi-party system means that some unlikely combinations can occur in specific questions. The prime example is on immigration, where the radical left parties and liberal parties have pushed for a more liberal policy than the Social Democrats and Moderates.

The leadership positions taken by the two women are also symptomatic of another trend in Sweden – female representation. Of the eight parties in parliament, four have female youth leaders and the Greens have male and female co-spokespeople. Irrespective of which side of the block divide the parties find themselves on, feminism and gender equality are big issues, with younger activists pushing their older colleagues to make changes.

'Feminism is a key bit of liberalism – it was Mary Wollstonecraft who started it all,' says Wagenius in reference to the English feminist pioneer and Nordic fan. 'There can be disagreements about what that means, but if people can feel comfortable calling themselves feminists that's a good thing.'

Being the head of a youth organisation is a full time job, paid for by the state. It involves going into schools, holding seminars and taking the message to the people, all with the blessing of the taxpayer.

'Firstly you have to go and try and get people involved in politics, but you also have to push the politics you believe in', explains Wagenius.

'You have to lead the organisation, influence the party and change society', adds Rasmusson. The party is the major frame of action in Swedish politics, with political groupings quick to co-opt new social movements when they arise. The electoral system means that one bad election can be a catastrophe for any particular party, and with such a range to choose from the older established parties cannot rely on loyal voters. At various times all parties bar the Social Democrats and Moderate party have flirted with losing their representation entirely.

At present it is the turn of Wagenius' Centre party to stare into the abyss. They are a long way from their heyday in the late 1970s and are still trying to come to terms with the end of rural life, replacing it with a robust countryside neo-liberalism under the leadership of its entrepreneurial young leader and avowed libertarian Annie Lööf.

Sweden's many parties, represented all the way from the European parliament down to local authorities, the church and the court system, are integral to the way its democracy works. Even the smaller ones have incomes of millions of pounds each year thanks to private investments and the comprehensive system of state subsidy. At present this is 450 million kronor a year, around 37 million pounds, divided amongst parliamentary parties and some groups in regional and local government.

This system is designed to liberate political parties from reliance on private interest groups and large scale private donors. In recent years though lobbying has become an increasingly important part of the Swedish political scene. In 2010 this came to a head when it was revealed that Svensk Näringsliv, Sweden's business interest organisation, had been paying former Social Democrats who had turned to PR consultancy as a way of influencing party policy.

Despite the rise of populist parties and the lobbying industry, the generously funded institutions of Sweden's democracy seem to be working; according to *The Economist*'s democracy index, Sweden is the fourth most democratic nation in the world. The country elects people using proportional lists, but each member also has a constituency for which they are responsible. There are 29, varying in size from south to north. As you go north Sweden generally gets redder, with different parties doing particularly well in different regions. Magda Rasmusson's place as a representative for Stockholm is mirrored in the party's strong presence in the capital. In recent years this spread of parties and voters has been complicated by huge demographic shifts within the country. Lightning quick urbanisation means that Stockholm plays an increasingly large role in deciding who ends up in power.

The proportionality of the Swedish system has become a defining characteristic of its model democracy, but the Social Democrats were originally in favour of a majority system of election like in the UK or US Congress. The proportional system was a result of the fact there were more than two parties in politics when universal suffrage was granted, and no one group was able to engineer dominance for itself. Conservatives and Liberals thus ensured representation even when the Social Democrats were securing huge electoral victories in the postwar period.

This diverse political mix means that Swedish politics is a complex interaction of multiple groups in a perpetual balancing act, in turn influenced by a ballooning number of think tanks, lobbyists and NGOs. It is this alliance building and triangulation that has come to define contemporary Swedish politics, and it was an alliance that would come to define the Swedish model's future.

* * *

The skies over the Baltic were blue as a tiny plane landed at Visby Airport on the Swedish island of Gotland. It was July 2006, and on board was the man destined to lead Sweden for the following eight years, Fredrik Reinfeldt. Next to him sat his party chairman and PR guru; Per Schlingmann is a man without whom eight years of Swedish history may well have been quite different. The two politicians from the Moderate party had a plan for their country, but to seize Sweden they had to begin their attack in the Baltic Sea.

As the plane taxied to a halt a few miles north of the Gotlandic capital, the mediaeval streets of the old fortress city were already busy with people. These were not just tourists though. For a week each summer Gotland becomes the destination of choice for the great and the good in Swedish politics and public life in an event that is part trade fair, part Riviera party, and a microcosm of Sweden's democracy.

This peculiar annual migration has its roots in a speech made by Olof Palme in 1968. Palme, shortly to be interviewed by David Frost and gunning for the party leadership, was jostling to take the reins at the peak of the Social Democratic party's dominance of 20th century Sweden. Holidaying on Gotland as he did every summer, he climbed onto the back of a lorry and began to address members of the public gathered in Almedalen, a park in the shadow of Visby's looming fortifications.

It was the beginning of an annual fixture that would put Gotland on the map, creating a tradition that has become a highpoint of the political calendar. Each year, the 'Almedalen Week' gives each of the eight parliamentary parties in the Swedish legislature a platform to discuss politics, unveil policies and sun themselves in the cool Baltic summer. This year they will be joined by a ninth in the form of the Feminist Initiative party, who previously held their own alternative Almedalen.

It was at Almedalen in 2006 that the Alliance for Sweden, a coalition of centre-right parties led by Reinfeldt, prepared itself for power. Under the expert guidance and branding of Schlingmann they created a united front to beat the Social Democrats and ruled for eight years, transforming the country in the process. It marked the beginning of a long winter for the left in Sweden, a period from which they have not yet fully emerged.

Gotland's landscape can be a harsh environment outside of summer. Off its northern tip lies the island of Fårö, where Ingmar Bergman chose to live in relative seclusion. His two films *Fårö Document* and *Fårö Document 1979* portray the yearly cycle of the landscape and its people, the end of the farming economy and an increasing sense of isolation from and friction with the modern world. With its pebble beaches, weather-beaten stacks and sea winds it transforms into a colourless landscape, the sea turning black under grey skies, icing as it hits the shore.

In July and August though the island's population explodes, no more so than in Almedal week. Flights and ferries are fully booked, finding a bed is nigh on impossible and the elite come out to play in the sunshine. The streets are filled with lobbyists, arms dealers, journalists, activists and politics junkies. They rub shoulders as they move from champagne receptions to speeches, with venues and groups in hot competition to attract the right kind of people to their event. In the space between the twilight and the dawn the lines become blurred and political colours mix.

In 2012 the Swedish rapper Timbuktu played a free set for the Green Party before their co-leader took to the stage to talk about climate change. In 2014 meanwhile, Per Schlingmann and the former Moderate International Aid Minister took part in an unintentionally hilarious outdoor DJ battle against their Social Democrat opposition rivals in the warm northern dusk. On the same latitude as northern Scotland, the light and warmth lingers and the bars close as the sun comes round again.

The sense of dislocation created by transplanting Stockholm to Gotland means that the rules change, the island becoming a dreamlike version of everyday politics. It is a self-consciously exclusive event, relying on the media to relay events back over the water to the mainland. Without this media presence the whole week would never reach many beyond the mix of politicians and representatives for the various organisations, agencies and campaigning groups actually present in Visby.

Almedalen is not, though, the week-long party its critics sometimes portray it as, at least not from a journalistic perspective. The politicians may be on holiday, but the journalistic corps has to be more attentive than ever. Equally so, outside of the wine receptions and after parties there are those less welcome in the sunny microcosm of the real Sweden created by the island. Unfortunately for those wishing to escape normal politics, the problems of contemporary Sweden are still present on Gotland.

The same Swedish pluralism that gives the country such a diverse political system means that the far right are now a fixture on the seminar lists and media schedules in Visby. The

13 per cent of the vote won by the Sweden Democrats means that they can no longer be ignored as a fringe group amongst the champagne, networking events and Q&AS. Within the neat borders of the island, the increasingly mainstream nature of extremist politics is all too plain to see. Having initially been referred to as a far-right party, the media has slowly normalised them to the point that they are now a firm part of the public consciousness. The Sweden Democrats have built themselves on nostalgia for a white Swedish golden age, and on an image of Sweden that is both insular and superior. According to the Swedish academic Maria Wendt though, associate professor in Politics at Stockholm University, nationalism is visible amongst all the parties in Gotland, beyond the brazen xenophobia of the Sweden Democrats.

'It strengthens the already symbiotic relationship between politicians and journalists... During Almedalen week, nationalism is always surprisingly prominent,' she has said of the event. 'Politicians and the media are strikingly unanimous in their belief that "we" are especially democratic, successful and equal in "our" nation.'

This exceptionalism in the national project is nothing new, and was already well established in Palme's time, as he stood atop a trailer in 1968. Although firmly internationalist, cultivating the idea of the people's home and talking about a particular Swedish way helped create the nation as a firmly delineated space. This dominant metaphor of family resulted in an inclusive civic nationalism in which all could work as one. It was this same phenomenon that let Fredrik Reinfeldt launch his Alliance for Sweden project in Gotland, standing not a trailer but on a carefully choreographed stage, a potential father of the nation like Palme before him. Swedish progress and Swedish exceptionalism go hand in hand, and no more so than in the idyllic surroundings of the Gotlandic summer.

Palme was to be mysteriously gunned down in the street in 1986 in an event that shook Sweden to the core. Who ordered him dead and why has never been ascertained, but his passing was the beginning of a long decline for Sweden's Social Democrats. Reinfeldt meanwhile departed quietly in September of 2014 after hemorrhaging votes to the far right.

What the future holds for Sweden's model democracy depends very much on who talks loudest and who can seize the agenda in the summers to come. In this brave new world, what plays out in the hyper-real political theatre of Visby has real consequences over the water in the remains of the people's home. Party membership is falling, but the electorate are still coming out in numbers to vote – at the last election 86 per cent of adult Swedes cast a ballot. The bigger question is what politics means to the new generation of young voters for whom Palme is an historical figure and the Social Democrats a shadow of their former selves, shorn of radicalism.

Whether in the parliamentary chamber, in its youth politics or in the Gotlandic sun, the public conversation is integral to making Sweden's democracy work. Looking out from the windows of the *Riksdag*, Hanna Wagenius issues a warning:

The biggest threat to democracy is that people won't engage. Our generation don't have an idea about how they might have to fight for things.

CHAPTER FOUR

A Feminist Utopia

How Sweden is halfway to equality

Speak to other women about your situation. You will discover that your problems are not private by shared by many; that they are created by the society in which we live.
GRUPP 8

THE WORDS OF encouragement penned by the feminist collective Grupp 8 are as true today as when they were written on a leaflet handed out to passers by in 1968. The eight original members of the organisation, which means Group 8 in English, were pioneers of the everyday equality Sweden has engineered with remarkable success. What this small group of feminist activists achieved can be linked directly with the high level of gender equality the country enjoys today. In the Sweden of the late 1960s politicians had gone a long way towards building their social democratic dream, but until a new wave of radicalism hit women's rights and feminism were still a secondary consideration for the Party.

The women of Group 8, many of whom would go on to become prominent public intellectuals or political figures, helped to lay the foundations for the eventual normalisation of gender politics in Swedish society. Group 8 became a symbolic focal point within the wider feminist movement, employing a strategy which focused on questions and demands that concerned a majority of women from all walks of life.

The founding members of the organisation first met whilst attending a pioneering class on gender and literature at Sweden's Uppsala university, run in the evenings because gender was not then deemed to be a valid subject by the university's literature department. From the original eight members it ballooned to become a widespread and widely recognised front. Local groups soon formed and a few years later over a thousand people participated in a march through the Swedish capital. Group-Eighters gatecrashed Trade Union rallies to highlight the inequality facing women at work, and drew attention to the lack of childcare by taking their children to see the head of Social Services at Stockholm city hall, letting them run around under the tables during the meeting. In 1972 a major conference was arranged at the Åsö Gymnasium school in Stockholm, packed to the rafters with inspired and eager activists in what is considered a turning point in the politicisation of Swedish women.

Low wages and poor working conditions saw women begin to protest en masse, with a wide range of feminist groups from various sectors of society cooperating in areas from childcare to the investigation of sexual offences and female unemployment. In the 1970s strikes by working-class women put the issue of female pay on the agenda, and by the end of the decade women had achieved real change in Sweden.

One of the Group-Eighters was a young literature scholar by the name of Ebba Witt-Brattström. Witt-Brattström was also pivotal in a new wave of action for equality in the 1990s that left an enduring mark on Sweden's political system; together with other leading activists she threatened to establish a new political party before the 1994 election in frustration at the slow pace of change by the large parties of left and right. In response the main political movers promptly adjusted their platforms and policies to be more inclusive. The women's slogan 'Half the power, all the wages' encapsulated their manifesto of 50–50 representation and parity of pay. Witt-Brattström would also be present at the founding of a real political party a few years later, one that is currently bringing a new kind of politics to Sweden, and to Europe. Almost half a century on from the radical pioneers of Group 8, their legacy and their attitude is intact in the form of a new generation of young women – and men – pushing the boundaries of gender.

* * *

'I have to be away by ten past so I can get the bus to the party,' says Gudrun Schyman, the charismatic co-leader of Sweden's Feminist Initiative party, as she glances at her tablet. In a small café down the street from the Swedish Parliament the veteran politician sits unassumingly in a corner, unrecognised by the tourists around her who flock to this part of old city.

The party she is referring to is a *homeparty*, a false Anglicism invented to describe the meetings of young activists across the country that have proven to be the pillar of a radical and increasingly successful feminist political movement with international ambitions. That night Schyman is booked to talk to a group of feminist supporters in Kungsholmen, an inner Stockholm suburb, merely one of many stops in a never-ending journey around the country.

Founded in 2005, these gatherings of young activists and supporters have been the cornerstone of Feminist Initiative, more usually known as Fi, in their rise from interesting also-rans to a small but significant force on Sweden's political scene.

'The concept came about by necessity,' says Schyman. 'Around the summer of 2013 there was a growing interest in feminism and Feminist Initiative. We had no money or resources and could not hire venues and the like, so I said "if you get 25 people at home I'll come." I'd tested it out in a European election previously with some success.'

The *homeparty* concept proved a winner. The idea is that someone else organises the event, which functions as way of lowering the thresholds for political participation.

'It is a great way to talk about issues in fairly relaxed circumstances,' Schyman adds. 'I started off doing evening things, and then spread into the afternoons, until finally we were doing breakfast meetings too.'

Until 2014 Fi were an enterprising but largely unrepresented minor party, famous for a clutch of celebrity backers such as Abba's Benny Andersson and the pop singer Robyn, as well as a high profile stunt in which they burned real money to highlight the gender wage gap. Their election campaign was based on hard work by the leadership and a huge number of miles covered, combined with a snappy campaign which made use of social media and tongue-in-cheek slogans such as 'Put the feminists in their place'. This was embodied by painted pink chairs placed on the street to symbolise parliamentary seats by party activists. Several Swedish indie bands even lent their music to an official Fi record. It was a masterful example of a new liquid politics that operated outside of traditional channels and took many by surprise.

The payoff for such innovation was a raft of seats in municipalities from the Swedish Arctic to the country's southern coast, as well as an MEP – the Roma human rights activist Soroya Post. The party narrowly missed out on seats in the Swedish parliament thanks to a four per cent barrier, but took home an admirable three per cent of the vote against the other better resourced parties.

Schyman says that the grass roots element was key to the campaign.

'It was an important element... we have been good with social media, largely out of necessity. Of all the parties in Sweden we have the highest profile on social media and that is where our members are, and that is their language.'

To people on the outside, gender-progressive Sweden might seem the last country in need of a feminist political party; Schyman and her colleagues are forthright about why they are needed though.

'Because we do not have a political party at this moment in time with a plan of how we achieve gender equality in the future and freedom from discrimination,' she says bluntly. 'There is no timetable. There's a parliamentary agreement that all the parties have signed up to with four goals, including equal views of parenthood and there have been a lot of nice words, but not much in the way of actual politics.'

Although the party itself began life as a campaign group, for Fi the plan is to gain power and enter parliament.

'We want in,' says Schyman. 'Above all else we want to liberate the particular areas of politics to do with human rights and "women's issues" which are often compartmentalised. Parties often have women's sections as if women are expected to be lobbyists in their own party, but that gets us nowhere. We need to take power. You can compare it to what the Greens did in Swedish politics in the '80s with sustainability. At the time that was not considered to be politics as it was not about class, and it took a while for them to get into parliament, but when they did everyone else was forced to sharpen up and the level of knowledge was raised. Today sustainability is taken for granted as part of everyday politics. That is what we will see with equality and human rights when we get in.'

The new perspective Fi are pushing is intersectional, postmodern politics. Asked about the party's priorities, Schyman is scathing about the reductive nature of most parties' campaigning.

'There are not three key points you can go to the polls with. Our aim is to see the connections and the context... the most important thing today is to see how it all fits together. The big mistake in most politics is not seeing this – how gender, class, ethnicity, sexuality and everything else is related, and there are power structures that perpetuate one another. That's the heart of the feminist analysis we have.'

The veteran leader has been here before. For a decade, until 2003, she was a popular leader of the Swedish Left Party. Now though, she thinks it is time for a different approach.

'That is a very old fashioned way to look at the whole thing. Left and right is just one measure and we need to develop democracy and politics and make sure there are other dimensions. Right now we have a strong focus in Europe and Sweden around the nation, tradition and norms, and on the other hand global human rights, critiquing these norms and social development. You have nationalism and feminism but with connections to other questions of power such as class and sustainability. All of these are related. It is these complexities that the traditional parties cannot really handle because they are stuck on that class-based left-right perspective. There is of course an awareness of structures in the Left and Social Democrats compared to the liberal feminist view of individual success, which changes nothing in the long term. We are concrete about the fact that these are structural problems which require social reforms, so it is easier to cooperate with the left-wing parties.'

For Fi to come this far has not been an easy ride, despite Schyman's experience. With little in the way of funds, the movement required huge sacrifices on the part of its activists and leading figures. Sissela Nordling Blanco, the Swedish-

Chilean activist who became Stockholm's human right's commissioner after 2014's election successes, has had to take a leave of absence due to the strain of working on a largely volunteer basis for the last three years. For a party that has stressed the 'invisible' unpaid work of women it is a bitter irony. Schyman has had a parliamentary pension to fall back on, but many of the party's younger members belong to an economically precarious group of young working women.

Despite the barriers to growth, the movement has already spawned imitators in Norway and Finland, whilst Schyman also points to the founding of the Women's Equality Party in the UK. The Norwegian party have already fielded candidates in Norwegian local elections autumn in Bergen and Oslo, Norway's two biggest cities.

Many of Feminist Initiative's members are young and newly engaged, but someone who has been part of the party's modest yet significant rise is Malin Sandqvist. In her mid-30s, she has been a member for a decade and lives in Värmdö, the suburban municipality covering Stockholm's sprawling green archipelago.

'For me it is a question of political pragmatism,' she says. 'I used to be a Left Party councillor where I came from and I felt something was missing – I was suspicious of Fi too to begin with because there was no class perspective and it took me a while before I really saw the intersectionality. I spoke to a good friend who was already a member and so I joined up. To begin with I saw it as a single-issue party and did not really see the relevance for things like public transport, but I think Gudrun has been a huge factor – she is something of a role model politically.'

Getting momentum rolling in a society that views itself as equal is a huge issue for Sandqvist and her fellow activists.

'There is this idea that we've come a long way and people

say stuff like "why should we complain?" she says. 'We have all the basics like rights to free abortions and childcare but that means we can dig a little deeper. People ask if we're not satisfied and we're not, because we're not finished yet. You can argue that these are luxury problems but I think it is a great sign that we have come this far and can afford to devote our time to luxury issues.'

By embedding itself in local politics and the European Parliament, Fi now has a base of activists and politicians to use as a springboard.

'I think the party will grow,' Sandqvist says hopefully. 'It's going slowly but next time round we'll have the means to run a completely different type of campaign. Then there's the fact the other parties have already started to pay attention to our politics – just the same as the Moderates have been dragged right [by the populist Sweden Democrats]. We're definitely not going to go backwards. In the councils where we have won seats we've proven we're more than just a gang of lunatics.'

This pragmatic feminism forms the basis of the Fi plan, and they hope they can appeal to people's everyday problems as much as an abstract sense of gender.

'I can vote for Fi for purely selfish reasons because their politics benefits me,' says Sandqvist, 'there are a lot of castles in the air and a lot of talk of strong women and that, but very few concrete measures.'

'I have four daughters, I need a society that works for me. I need working public transport, good schools... and welfare questions are important to me. And with my four daughters, with them in mind it simply has to get better.'

With their movement growing and a new wave of politicised young people across Europe wondering where gender equality went wrong, Fi hope that they can make a lasting impression and turn pink into a regular fixture alongside red, blue, yellow and green on the political map. The real challenge will be whether their postmodern politics can compete with the power structures of old.

What Fi's appearance illustrates is that progress on gender equality in Sweden has been far from consensual even after the important changes of the '60s new wave. Violence against women is still a problem, and in the European elections the Sweden Democrats went into battle under the slogan 'Stop the extreme feminism', illustrated by an election broadcast featuring ethnically Swedish girls hanging out together and asserting their right to 'just be women'. As it has chalked up its victories Swedish feminism has also seen a violent backlash.

Maria Sveland, a prominent Swedish novelist and columnist, experienced this gender kickback first hand. After achieving success in Sweden and the wider world with her novel *Bitter Bitch*, a piece of auto-fiction pointing out the injustices in the supposedly happy and equal Swedish nuclear family, she was subject to sustained anti-feminist abuse by an emboldened group of armchair warriors With the resurgence of the populist right this increased, and Sveland found herself labelled part of an ill-defined blob of 'cultural Marxists' in the crosshairs of a self-proclaimed resistance movement. Spurred on by the abuse, she documented her experience of anti-feminism in a book, concluding that 'Whether liberation movements have been about gender, race, class, ethnicity, sexual orientation or religion, what they have in common is the fact they have never won their rights without a struggle.

This was something that Group 8 and other pioneering feminists knew all too well. A huge plank of the original platform for Group 8 and its offshoots was the recognition of the specific needs of women, and high on the list of basic demands was childcare. By 1970 only five per cent of pre-school children had a place in nursery. Abortion was severely limited too, and it was not until 1974 that free abortions were allowed at the request of the mother without medical justification – even if you did not want a child, your body was not entirely your own. In a reverse of today's situation, women would travel to communist Poland if they could not get the approval of a doctor for the procedure.

The year after abortion laws were relaxed, those with children could also take advantage of nursery care provided by the local authority, and in the same 12 months maternity pay for women was replaced with parental insurance, laying the grounds for a more gender equal division of childcare that would allow men to stay at home and women to return to work. It meant that the Swedish model was slowly but surely becoming equal, whether some people liked it or not

* * *

In the library of Stockholm University Elin Nordström is leant over a desk. She is studying for her exams to become a teacher at a Swedish pre-school, the mix of nursery and primary school that has become synonymous with the global view of Swedish childcare.

Built in the early 1970s, the Stockholm University campus is an exercise in functional planning set in open parkland on the city's north side. When the buildings were first erected the Swedish model had not yet grown to include one of its most famous achievements, but today it educates hundreds of new students each year in how to teach in a pre-school, or *förskola*.

The international press regularly write about Sweden's childcare arrangements, most famously when a gender-neutral pre-school opened on Stockholm's city centre for the children of largely upper class parents, passing exception off as typicality. The story attracted write-ups by the BBC, the *New York*

Times, The Guardian and a host of other international news outlets, and the trope was repeated through photo montages of designer Swedish fathers spending time with their children on click driven web media.

Despite the stories of transgressive gender-free education, the experience of childcare for most people is comfortably banal. From its earliest days, a key part of Sweden's modern women's movement was the general recognition that until the childcare question was solved and women were liberated from the home, they would forever be second class to men. 'Good free nursery care and afterschool care for all children' was not just a rallying slogan, but the most important step in emancipating women from the domestic sphere and tackling discrimination on the labour market.

'We talk a lot about the social aspects where children can learn to socialise at an early stage, but there is that other point about the pre-school system being an important part of Swedish equality,' says Nordström. 'Up until the '60s people could not work and look after kids, and until then it was just the children of the upper class who would be taken care of, what you called a *barnträdgård*.' The word literally means children's garden, or kindergarten. 'Now though we have a much more democratic system,' she adds.

Since the 1970s the childcare system has been transformative for working women, but has also been transformed into an educational tool in its own right. Children in Sweden do not start school until age seven, so the pre-school years are an important part of their development. Attendance is not entirely free, and varies slightly from area to area within certain pre-defined limits. In Stockholm it costs 1260 kronor a month for full time attendance, just under 100 pounds. It then decreases with each child, and reductions are available for lower earners. It means that the money gained from working is not entirely wiped out by the cost of childcare. More than a playgroup, pre-school is supposed to stimulate and develop children rather than just keeping them out of harm's way.

This is partly why the people who work in them have to be much better qualified than simple babysitters. To become a pre-school teacher you have to study for three years, taking in a range of subjects and passing university exams like for any other profession. The framework allows certain key values and issues to be pushed, including gender equality. International reports of genderless children might be somewhat exaggerated, but consideration of gender is built into the curriculum from an early stage.

'An awareness of gender and how you counter traditional gender roles is part of the teaching plan,' Nordström enthuses. 'There's always some kind of gender perspective present. When we take maths modules for example we look at how maths is normally viewed as a male field and the expectations you have about boys being good at maths. It is more or less built in to everything we read.'

Far from being the aggressive eradication of identity its critics would portray it as, the awareness of gender issues in children's early years education is designed to give them equal opportunities and ambitions. Pre-school is open to all children in Sweden from two years old. The final year of pre-school is designed to function as a bridge to prepare children for entry to primary education.

'We have a different curriculum to what they have in schools,' explains Nordström. 'In school the curriculum is based around achieving specific things, but in pre-school it is not goal oriented. The whole point is that it should be fairly democratic and the children get to explore science and maths but through other channels. Play is really important, as is developing language.'

As part of their pre-school years children are taken out and about in the local community, with their days structured but not forcefully so. It is not uncommon to run into a group of pre-schoolers in high visibility jackets shuffling through suburbs or riding three abreast on a pushchair. Nordström is evangelical about her chosen line of work.

'I think it is important,' she says. 'The system is pretty unique in that it is open to all kids and costs almost nothing. There are private pre-schools as well but ours are council run, and they take 98 per cent of all kids who grow up in Sweden. That means that it is unusual not to put your child into pre-school, which is one of the key aspects.'

Nordström will soon be finished and start working full time, and like millions of other women across Sweden she need not stop if she wants to have children. The comprehensive system that Sweden has put in place is not universally loved though. The Christian Democratic Party, together with sections of some of the other more conservative parties on the political spectrum, have accused the childcare system of reducing choice and taking children out of the home. Where they have had influence they have pushed for a care benefit that pays parents to stay at home instead of sending their child to pre-school. In an especially Swedish appropriation of the language of freedom and choice, freedom to work has been superseded by the struggle for the freedom not to.

Such resistance to Sweden's institutionalised systems of equality play into foreign ideas about the country's shady statist agenda, a McCarthyite obsession that is regularly given voice on conservative media elsewhere. Jan Sjunesson, editor of the ultra-conservative newspaper *Samtiden* with links to the far right, authored a book on the subject that pandered to stereotypes and sought to expose the dark truth behind Sweden's social engineering. Translated into English, it was lapped up by American libertarians and eager critics of the Swedish model. It mentioned the childcare system as just one element in its dystopian vision of an experiment gone wrong, a state out of control where political correctness was enforced from morning to nightfall. Unfortunately for Sjunesson and the other brave crusaders of libertarian freedom, the majority of Swedes are extremely satisfied with this particular addition to the Swedish model.

* * *

The childcare system may have helped Swedish women out of the house and into the workplace, but this was not the only obstacle to gender equality. Getting women to work is one thing, but making sure they enjoy the same conditions as men is a challenge only half met. On the other side of Sweden, up a narrow wooded valley in the suburbs of Gothenburg, feminist politics is being put into practice in a different way to the everyday equality of pre-school and the radical politics of Feminist Initiative.

The Svartedalen care home on the island of Hisingen – better known as home to a factory for Volvo cars and the football team BK Häcken – sits at the end of one of the city's sprawling tram lines, the small blue and white cars on constant circulation from the city centre and back again past wooden houses and concrete high rises. Down the hill from the tram stop and hidden behind a wall of flats, the building sits in leafy isolation from the city, providing publicly funded care for those unable to look after themselves.

In Svartedalen though the story is less about the residents and more about the staff. In a move reported (and misre-ported) globally Sweden's second city has been carrying out a pioneering experiment in the way people work – by giving council employees shorter working days with full pay. At Svartedalen the care workers are now free to leave two hours earlier each shift, but earn the same amount as before.

How this relates to feminism is not immediately clear, at least not until you look around the Svartedalen corridors. A vast majority of the staff are female, and so the workforce is subject to the same structural inequalities that divide men and women across Europe. Despite progress on reducing gender inequality, women in Sweden earn on average 17 per cent less than men. They are also more likely to take on strenuous work in the healthcare sector, and to have jobs that require repetitive tasks. A report from Gothenburg's Sahlgrenska hospital found that women were taking higher numbers of sick days, taking longer to recover and had worse health as a result. It was a problem repeated across the country, but one that barely registered on the radar of mainstream, middle class gender debates.

This invisible labour posed a problem, so the local authority decided to try out an innovative solution. The experiment at Svartedalen is a flagship policy for the Swedish Left Party, governing together with the Social Democrats and Green Party on Gothenburg's city council. Elderly care is the responsibility of the local authority, so the coalition determined to use it as a testbed for their experiment with working women.

Only a few months into the trial, the staff at Svartedalen were already reporting great results, according to Charlotte Jern, head of one of the care units.

'People had been discussing it for a while, but after the local elections in the autumn of 2014 we got the green light [...] The positive effects are obvious and the people who work here seem to have a new energy and drive,' she says.

The effect of Svartedalen's innovation was being felt by residents too. Staff who worked closely with dementia sufferers reported that those in their care responded positively to more relaxed staff. The experiment, begun in the February of 2015, was immediately extended.

'The residents want more time too. They say that the staff seem much less hurried and more calm now. That is probably the best effect,' says Jern of the widely lauded scheme.

The realities faced by Jern and her staff are the unseen edge of the struggle for gender equality, away from the metropolitan opinion pages and academic discussions. Working women underpin the healthcare system in Sweden, the irony being that other people's wellbeing can come at the cost of their own.

In their bright office at Gothenburg's City Hall, sat firmly on the main square as the trams rumble by on their way from Svartedalen to the other side of the city, Alice Vernersson and Daniel Bernmar are pleased with their pet project. Looking less like local politicians than graphic designers – Bernmar has a cardigan and moustache combination that is upstaged only by Vernersson's clipped blonde hair – they are proud to be putting into practice a policy that has drawn journalists from all over the world and which they genuinely believe will make a difference to the lives of municipal employees

'We have researchers monitoring it the whole time. It is expensive, but today we have a situation where we pay for our elderly care and welfare with women's work and physical health as they wear themselves out,' says Bernmar seriously.

The Gothenburg trial cost 8.2 million kronor – around 700,000 pounds – but is money well spent according to Bernmar and Vernersson. Bernmar is a so-called *Borgaråd*, akin to a council convener, and Vernersson is his deputy. Together they are responsible for the city's elderly care and the care units where the trial is taking place. It is a tiny portfolio in one single authority in a medium sized country, but they are still aiming high.

'This is just a pilot project, but it will hopefully form the basis of a bigger discussion of how we work,' says Bernmar, whose party have sought to profile themselves as the inheritors of Sweden's radical approach to working conditions. 'Male professions have been mechanised to become less strenuous, but for women there is still a lot of hard work. Elderly care is one of those areas. One of the ways we have maintained care is through lower levels of pay and working conditions, and we want to get away from that.'

As the two politicians chat over coffee in their office the project has been running for just over a month, and there is an aspiration to roll it out across all public employers in Sweden's second city, though popular contrary to international reports the innovative approach is still the exception rather than the rule. To properly gauge the impact of the change, the study has been replicated at a nearby care home of similar size with the old eight hour working model. The results have been monitored on a continuous basis to gain an understanding of the exact effects of shorter days, and researchers have focused on the health of the staff, the wellbeing of the patients and the overall potential effect on employment. The same model is also being tried out at a hospital on the other side of the city, whilst a car servicing plant nearby has successfully run six hour days voluntarily for a number of years. The plant claims that it has reduced sick leave whilst the hospital has employed the tactic as a way of reducing staff turnover and burnout.

Not everyone is happy with Gothenburg's innovative approach though. Opposition parties in the city branded the experiment a waste of public resources, arguing that it was not for the taxpayer to subsidise free time off. The Moderates were firmly opposed to Bernmar's work and the city's attempt to manipulate the labour market. This kind of opposition to structural intervention is a point of view that cuts down the middle of Swedish feminism – on the one hand it is about empowering women to be as successful as their male counterparts, on the other about changing the very structures of society to better reflect the needs of a majority of the population. What both sides can agree on is that there is still much to be done.

What the experiment in Svartedalen shows is the degree to which feminism and an awareness of gender has become a mainstream concern in contemporary Swedish politics. Far from being innate, Sweden has succeeded in popularising and then embedding an awareness of gender inequality as both a moral and practical question across the political spectrum. The country has come on a journey from the pioneers of the suffrage moment to the mass movements of the 1960s, the gender-aware 1990s and finally the renewed feminist politics of the present day. Whereas early feminists sought to find a balance and virtue in being a woman, the debate has now begun transcend such essentialism and is finding new outlets and perspectives.

Nina Björk is one of Sweden's best known female intellectuals and has been an important voice in contemporary debates on how and why gender inequality arises. An academic, writer and journalist, in the mid-1990s she wrote a groundbreaking book called *Under the pink Duvet* which popularised the concept of gender performativity in Sweden – the idea that gender roles are assigned and acted – in which she attacked the idea that equality was simply about balancing men and women.

'I have criticised the dream of a woman as the utopia of feminism', wrote Björk, 'yet I have pushed my own dream, a utopia; the dream that a person might not have their identity and purpose determined by their sex.' It is a view of feminism based on a very liberal idea of the person rather than any desire to essentialise the feminine, and one increasingly acknowledged as legitimate.

Björk's liberal view sits alongside other diverse shades and perspectives on gender equality in modern Sweden. Whilst Feminist Intitiative are at the radical edge of gender equality in contemporary Sweden, feminism takes many different forms, some highly visible and some hidden away in the side valleys of suburban care homes. All of them though are moving in the same direction, and in a critical mass that has pushed and dragged the country forward step by step.

In 2014 the Swedish government, under the leadership of Margot Wallström, went public with a project that would draw praise and derision in equal measure – its feminist foreign policy. It provoked consternation on the comment pages of political magazines and seemed to confirm the worst suspicions of the world's eager watchers of state mandated equality. Spearheaded by Wallström and her Green counterpart Isabella Lövin, it tried to put theory into practice and turn rhetoric into reality in a way that meant challenging bastions of male dominance at home as well as overseas.

After the awkward questions posed to Wallström in the *Riksdag* on weapons exports and internal struggles with the grand old men of the Social Democrats, in the spring of 2015 Sweden finally cancelled its arms treaty with Saudi Arabia over human rights abuses and gender inequality. It is possible to pick holes in Sweden as a feminist utopia, but gender politics is one area of the Swedish model ripe for export.

CHAPTER FIVE

Svennotopia

The struggle for Swedishness

There is no one particular place that is Sweden.
OLOF PALME

'ZLATAN ISN'T SWEDISH,' says Mattias Karlsson in what should be a straightforward interview with the publicly run Swedish Radio. There is incredulity in the studio as the immigration spokesperson for the Sweden Democrats is asked to explain himself by the show's host. It is 2007 and the Sweden Democrats are still getting used to the media limelight, radio interviews included.

'I do not perceive him as Swedish,' elaborates Karlsson. For a party that stresses loyalty to Sweden as a key part of nationality, who is Swedish and who is not is a significant preoccupation. The main obstacle to Karlsson's logic is that Zlatan Ibrahimovic is one of the key players for Sweden's national football team, and nowadays its captain too. Born, like many others, to a Balkan immigrant family, the gangly Paris St Germain forward is one of the best players the country has ever seen. More remarkably, Karlsson went on to add that Henrik Larsson, the Celtic legend whose father is from the Cape Verde islands and who preceded Ibrahamovic as the figurehead of the national team, was Swedish because he behaved in a sufficiently 'Swedish' way. In the bizarre world of post-racial far-right politics, nationality has become more subjective than ever.

Karlsson is only a few years older than Zlatan, both of them raised in southern Sweden where the cities are red and the countryside blue, and nowadays the far-right's yellow too. They represent different ideas about what being Swedish mean, and both are no stranger to national symbolism. On the subway platforms of Stockholm, a series of Volvo adverts portray the football star in a snowy landscape with a hunting rifle, conquering the Nordic wilderness in an aesthetic remarkably similar to the Sweden Democrats' own ideas on Swedish masculinity.

The rise of the far right in Sweden has forced the country to confront its self-image and the friction between the Scandinavia of the imagined past and the interdependent complexities of global modernity. As Left Party activists shouted 'no racists on our streets' to the TV cameras on election night in 2014, Karlsson and his party colleagues were celebrating what they thought was the beginning of a national awakening. Björn Söder, the parliamentary speaker, had as recently as 2009 addressed a rally in the town of Ljungbyhed near Malmö with the call to arms 'Sweden for the Swedes', letting the mask slip from the TV-friendly and publicly presentable new Sweden Democrats. The great unanswered question behind the applauding party members in front of Söder though was who the Swedes really are. When David Frost sat down to interrogate Olof Palme in 1969, the Prime Minister-to be's answer that there was no one place that was Sweden was both diplomatic and earnestly honest.

Even in the late 1960s Sweden was a diverse country with large immigrant groups from Finland and southern Europe. In the golden years of the social democratic project people came to work in Sweden's factories, as refugees from the ruins of postwar Europe or as fugitives from the authoritarian regimes of the Eastern Bloc. Alongside its own internal diversity

Sweden acquired a raft of new citizens from all corners of the world, and they kept coming. In 1973 the US-backed coup in Chile and the death of President Salvador Allende saw a wave of refugees from South America, followed in 1979 by Iranians fleeing the Islamic revolution. They were in turn followed by Iraqis escaping war in the 1980s, Somalians and a steady stream of Kurds from Syria, Turkey and Iraq without a state to call home. Most recently, thousands fleeing the conflict in Syria have found their way to Sweden's shores. Without a large empire in its recent past, immigration in modern Sweden is a human map of 20th and early 21st century's conflicts.

Contemporary Sweden is a paradox, on the one hand wearing its nationality explicitly, on the other positioning itself as an open and forward looking country for whom nationalism is an obstacle to global progress. On public holidays small Swedish flags fly from municipal buses and trams, and trade unions mount advertising campaigns stressing the virtues of the Swedish model compared to the world outside. Internationally too, Sweden is distilled into its parts. The front page of Sweden's official website offers visitors lead articles on migration (rather than immigration), Swedish film, gender equality, an introduction to 'the Swedish kitchen' and a breakdown of the country's supposed love affair with nature. The promotional images show people of different ethnic backgrounds, but all portrayed with the same bright, well-dressed aesthetic. In the filtered world of national branding Swedishness becomes consensual and de-politicised, though like anywhere in contemporary Europe the reality is somewhat more complex.

* * *

The snow is beginning to drift against the chain-link fence that separates the railway line from the woods in the Stockholm suburb of Flemingsberg, a new-build satellite town a short ride by commuter train from Stockholm's central station. The thermometer is below zero and people gaze out from the centrally heated apartment blocks that dominate the valley onto the road and railway below. From the ticket hall of the railway station students ascend the huge enclosed escalator that keeps them out of the February chill to the campus of Södertörn University, a mix of down jackets and rucksacks moving slowly up the hillside.

At the other end of the platforms, a woman in a head-scarf carrying a blue IKEA bag stuffed with cushions heads off from the station's back entrance, turning between the hoardings of a building site and a yard for industrial machinery. As she walks off down the icy cycle path her destination is an abandoned bridge abundment stacked with caravans and wooden shacks. Improvised chimneys kick wood smoke out into the frigid winter air. This little parade of homes houses around 40 Roma migrants, many of whom are busy trying to shift a trailer that has slipped in the freezing and thawing mud.

One of the people with their weight under the metal caravan is Elvis, a 23 year old member of the Roma community dressed in a woolly hat and thick jacket to fight off the cold. The moniker is a nickname he has adopted as he has moved across Europe to make himself more easily identifiable – Elvis Presley was supposedly descended from Roma migrants to the US. This Elvis arrived in Sweden via Germany, and switching between English, Swedish, German and Romanian, he talks about how he and his family came to be in the tiny ramshackle encampment on the edge of a planned Nordic suburb.

'We're all from Romania. We have come to Sweden to earn money, but it is hard to find a job,' he says, gesturing at the crowd of people huddled behind him. It is a simple but true story. Instead of working, most of the people at the camp get by through begging in Stockholm's inner city. Coming for a few months at a time, they can then take what they make back to their families in Romania. In Sweden's new Roma communities, children are conspicuous by their absence, featuring only on laminated plastic cards where the migrants beg for money.

'It gets too cold. We live in the caravans together where it is warmer,' he says. With the temperature usually well below zero, being outside any length of time in the long Nordic winter is not pleasant. He gestures toward the nearest caravan, wood smoke trailing from its roof, and opens the door, presenting the other members of his family. Inside, a group of mostly older men and women are sprawled across the tiny space, including Elvis' father.

'He lost his leg in an accident,' Elvis says, pointing to a bearded figure in a home-knitted cardigan. The big man on the improvised sofa pulls up his trouser leg to reveal where it stops just below the knee. The injury is the result of an industrial accident suffered whilst working illegally in Eastern Europe, they claim. The inside of the caravan is cosy, heated by the wooden embers in a stove added to the vehicle by some ingenious spatial improvisation. Outside, the express trains zip past on the main line from Stockholm to Gothenburg, Oslo and Copenhagen. This particular camp is one of the more homely, with many Roma reduced to spending the night curled up amongst the concrete pillars of Stockholm's empty motorway underpasses and subway stations.

The existence of camps like the one in Flemingsberg, and the people who live in them, has become an increasingly divisive issue in Sweden and symptomatic of its larger attempts to grapple with a balance of moral responsibility and practical need. Legally entitled to be there but often deeply unwelcome,

Sweden's Roma are caught in limbo and expose the divisions in rhetoric and reality that the country must face. Citizens mostly of Romania, they fit into neither the EU ideals of skilled mobile labour, nor into the diverse group of political and economic migrants whom Sweden's generous asylum policies seek to aid.

Sweden's highly regulated housing market with very few private lets means that finding even low grade housing is difficult. Access to its institutions and bureaucracy often requires a social security number and finding long-term housing from outwith the system can be difficult for non-Swedes with better linguistic and financial positions than these Eastern European migrants. The same is true for non-emergency aspects of healthcare. As a result, those arriving in Sweden without financial means are forced onto an unregulated black market or compelled to live in temporary camps like the one that has sprung up in the Flemingsberg snow. Several other similar communities had been torn down in the months before by bailiffs and the police, shifting their residents between local municipalities.

Sweden has pursued a strongly integrationist agenda to migration, in recent years extending to higher demands on language learning for new arrivals in politically motivated responses to perceived divisions. It also recruits skilled immigrants to its research and healthcare sectors, including large numbers of educated middle-class refugees from the Balkans and Middle East. Most recently, the ongoing conflict in Syria has led to an increase in the number of people travelling to the country for temporary or permanent refuge, joining the already large Syrian community. The wave of Roma from the EU are just the latest influx of the various peoples to find their way north.

People of Roma ethnicity have lived in Sweden for hundreds

of years and are officially a national minority, enjoying certain legal protections to language and support for culture.

The reality, though, is somewhat at odds with the stated aspirations of the government. Roma children underperform in school and structural discrimination is common. The group were only allowed to enter the education system in the 1960s and knowledge of Roma culture in Sweden is still low despite legal protection. Maria Leissner, the head of a board on Roma issues appointed by the last Swedish government, described their situation in Sweden as 'worse than a developing country'. In a scathing report she outlined how fewer than half of all Roma children in Sweden attend school, not including the newly arrived EU Roma who are invisible to the state.

In 2014 Niklas Orrenius, a journalist for the leading Swedish newspaper *Dagens Nyheter*, revealed the existence of a database of more than 4,000 people with a Roma background compiled by the police. The database included children and pensioners and was an example of 'the last sanitised racism' according to Orrenius.

Despite the long legacy of Roma in Scandinavia, the most prominent in the public eye are still the newly arrived EU migrants. At the beginning of 2015 the governing Conservative and Progress parties in neighbouring Norway attempted to introduce legislation that would have banned begging anywhere in the country and criminalised people giving beggars help. In theory, it would have applied to all begging, but critics argued that its link to Roma migration was obvious. The legislation was eventually withdrawn after criticism from churches, opposition politicians and the Council of Europe.

Like elsewhere on the continent, Sweden has a chequered history in its treatment of the ethnic group. In 1948, a riot in Jonköping led to vigilantes hunting travelling Roma and attacking their homes, encouraged by local press and a passive police force. More recently, individual politicians in the Swedish Conservative party have voiced support for criminalisation of begging, and the Sweden Democrats posted adverts in Stockholm's metro system with the slogan 'stop organised begging' during their local election campaign. The dissonance between the good-hearted, generous Sweden of popular perception and this deeply closed society is tangible.

On a Monday afternoon, the white tiled passage linking Stockholm's central station and the metro hub next door is thick with people rushing from overground to underground. As they stream along the corridor it is the people not moving who stand out. Commuters keen to catch their trains are met by a human wall selling mobile phone sim cards, handing out flyers and, most noticeably, begging for money from the floor of the hallway. Holding laminated signs with pictures of their family and stutteringly translated pleas in English and Swedish, the Roma trying to earn money are hard to miss. Many of the people running to the metro will already have encountered them on the local trains where they patrol carriages and will probably encounter them again on the metro. The passage is a prime position – not only is it full of people, but it also offers some respite from the bitterly cold weather. Nowhere does the well-paid whiteness of Stockholm's metroland clash as visibly with the situation of these migrants as here.

Another person standing still in the crowd is Sven Hovmöller. A semi-retired chemistry professor at Stockholm University and a Social Democrat in local government, he is the vice-president of HEM, a volunteer group that collects clothes and provides what help it can to Sweden's Roma. *Hem* is Swedish for home, but the acronym is symbolic in another way too. It stands for Homeless EU Migrants, the name with which activists have sought to humanise Romanian Roma and highlight the huge inequality in access to help compared to other immigrants from the EU. Less sympathetically inclined Swedes refer to the newly arrived simply as 'the beggars'.

In his rucksack Hovmöller has a stack of magazines and printed paper slips in Romanian explaining what he is doing.

'The idea is that they should sell the magazine instead of begging. They can make between two and five times as much,' he says with enthusiasm. The veteran Social Democrat has only been working with HEM since last spring, but is now fully engaged in the project. As he willfully admits, he was as ignorant of the Roma as most other people before they became a regular sight on Swedish streets.

'You see beggars, you wonder what's up and what their story is, so I went out to one of the camps where they were living and got to see how poor they were. It started by taking them water and making sanitary facilities. Now we organise Swedish classes every Sunday. These are EU migrants who can't get any help at all. Occasionally they might get a place to sleep,' he says. In the coldest months of November and December, when temperatures plummet, churches across Sweden opened their doors to provide temporary shelter. Sleeping outside in Sweden in winter without the right protection is lethal.

'The state could open a place for them to stay, just like with other refugees,' thinks Hovmöller. 'They are refugees from a thousand years of oppression and racism. Illiteracy is high, so they are in a worse situation than many of the people who come here from Africa, for example.' This is the fundamental sticking point for Sweden's Roma. According to the European Union none of its member states have conditions bad enough that its citizens can claim asylum in others. Nobody knows exactly how many EU Roma have come to Sweden either. Hovmöller gives an estimate of a few thousand, but even the authorities have little idea.

The idea of the pamphlet Hovmöller is distributing is to change the way people interact with Roma and to give some context to why they have come to Sweden. It is a similar strategy to that taken by Felicia Iosif, a Romanian Roma immigrant to Sweden, and Sara Olausson, an illustrator and comic writer. After meeting in the Stockholm suburb of Liljeholmen, the two became friends and produced a book, Felicia, about the background of Roma migrants across Europe using Iosif's own experiences.

Sitting in the white sterile premises of a coffee chain in a municipal shopping centre, Olausson waves to another Roma woman she knows passing by. Further along the pristine white mall, two women perch charging their budget mobile phones from the sockets intended for the arcade's vacuum cleaners.

'We told each other about our lives and we couldn't speak each other's languages, but you can communicate. With the help of a Romanian friend we translated and got Felicia's story out,' says Olausson. It is a project built on the understanding that if you can grasp someone else's culture you can help them to integrate. Iosif had already travelled back to Romania, and Olausson was about to join her. It would be Olausson's fourth trip to visit the members of the Swedish Roma families who stay at home, with the children left behind the subject of a new series of comics through which Swedish children can learn about their Roma peers. Part of this involves tackling the stereotypes about Roma perpetuated by populist media outlets and online, she says.

'I was lucky enough to already have a publisher, and to tell her story we had to go there… you hear about big palaces in the media and there are indeed some beautiful houses that families build, but inside it is just as poor as everywhere else. Racists use this as proof, but these are people who have never commanded respect at home. It is understandable that some of them might like to live in a good house, like anybody else.'

The last few years have seen an explosion in an alternative, and largely web-based, right-wing media in Sweden. Making use of Facebook and other social media, stories with vague sources from respectable-sounding outlets spread quickly but silently with just a few clicks. This, believes Olausson, is the real battleground – to get both the public and politicians to better understand how and why Roma have come to end up on Stockholm's streets. This balance of cultural understanding and economic assistance is tricky, though.

'Sweden has come a long way, but just as the goodwill has increased, so has the hate,' says Olausson, ominously. Another female activist working to integrate newly arrived Roma was forced to stop media engagement because of threats and misogynist hate speech. Olausson herself was manhandled by bailiffs when trying to rescue clothes and blankets from a Roma camp being torn down by the authorities. It is a perfect storm of anti-immigration sentiment, a disdain for women and a misanthropic approach to humanity.

In 2014 a Romanian government minister courted controversy when she visited Sweden to discuss migration and claimed that Roma were not discriminated against in their home country. A changing Europe and changing domestic politics in Sweden meanwhile mean that even in a society viewed as a model of tolerance and integration, old prejudices have re-emerged. As they have become increasingly visible, the Roma have also become an easy target for Sweden's resurgent populist right. As well as soaring to new heights in the national parliament, September 2014 also saw the Sweden Democrats take their first seats in Stockholm's city hall following their highly visible anti-begging campaign, plastered on buses and across the metro system. Their rallying cry is the innocent sounding 'Security and tradition'.

In her centrally heated and publicly funded office Maria Danielsson sips a cappuccino on the sofa, surrounded by her American college diploma and photos of her family. The group leader for the Sweden Democrats in Stockholm switches between California soccer-mom English and Swedish as she explains why the party think a begging ban is needed.

'The begging issue has gone from somewhat problematic to immensely problematic... it is causing problems with sanitation. We're the only party in Stockholm that wants to ban begging,' she says with a sense of both pride and concern. It is a familiar line, in which the problem of immigration is reiterated as concern for the problems of immigrants.

Danielsson goes to pains to point out that she and her party have nothing against Roma immigration, but claims that it is not Sweden's job to deal with the 'systematic problem' created by poverty in Eastern Europe.

'I have members of my own party and others contacting me and saying "I am tired of this, I want to hit them", and people are pushing them around.' In the logic of the Sweden Democrats, immigration rather than ignorance causes racism. Danielsson is herself an immigrant twice over, first from Sweden to America and then back again.

Her political beliefs aside, Danielsson is a fairly typical suburban mother, and she does not think that her party or politics are being treated fairly, yet the Swedish media is dominated by discussions of immigration. In November 2014 when the Sweden Democrats very nearly toppled the government by backing the opposition budget, the centre-right parties discovered a renewed enthusiasm for populist policies such as language tests and benefit limits. Her arguments are familiar, the same ones used all over Europe by the insurgent nationalist movements making themselves felt on the continent.

'We want to be able to be nationalist without being called fascist, and talk about immigration without being called racist,' she says in a slightly hurt voice. 'I would actually say that right now Sweden is not a democracy.' The fact that one of her party colleagues chairs parliamentary sessions does not make her question her conclusion. Democracy is a malleable term for the Sweden Democrats; in the spring of 2015 she was the victim of an attempted internal coup, only to be saved by the party leadership under the direction of Mattias Karlsson. The party is led by a gang of four powerful men intent on becoming national leaders, and they control the party with an iron discipline whenever their project is threatened.

Like the men at the top, Danielsson has ambitions for the Sweden Democrats to become the biggest party and form a government that 'puts Sweden first'. Her role model is Norway and the success achieved by the anti-immigration Progress party. All four of the mainland Scandinavian countries have seen the growth of such parties, with the Danish People's Party and the True Finns in Finland also commanding support on a populist message of 'economic realism', cultural exceptionalism and resistance to globalisation. The Sweden Democrats, though, are unique among the four in emerging from the traditional white power movement.

Not all members of the Sweden Democrats are as diplomatic as Danielsson. Previously, candidates have described Roma in Sweden as a 'cancer' and the party has engaged in a process described by Danielsson as 'cleansing' to expel its most outwardly racist members. Even without the Sweden Democrats, Sweden can be a tough society for newcomers. It is the ultimate irony that a system specifically designed to provide security for the majority acts as a barrier to the integration of those outside it. Both the previous and current Swedish governments meanwhile have stated their opposition to racism and emphasised the place of Roma as one of the country's officially recognised national minorities, but words are only half the story.

The Minister for Culture and Democracy, Alice Bah Kuhnke, was plunged into the maelstrom of complex cultural politics as soon as she assumed office, but her government are in a weak position to do anything significant without a full majority. The question of whether restating a commitment to multiculturalism can solve the complex structural inequalities affecting Swedish and EU Roma remains largely unanswered. Swedish civil society has begun to show a will to understand its suddenly prominent minority, but the real test will be whether the Swedish government can reach a solution different to the ones being touted by populist politicians across Europe, and whether the model can be made not just to hold, but to hold those for whom it was not designed.

* * *

The winters may be hard for outsiders in Sweden, but in the height of summer Sweden's national identity shows itself most clearly. It is Midsummer in the southern province of Småland, a picturebook landscape of deep forests and small farms a few hours south of Stockholm. According to the tourist brochures and stereotypes the festival is as Swedish as it gets. Traditional food, dancing around poles and family meetups are *de rigueur*, so much so that expat communities around the world have their own midsummer parties in the depths of the southern winter. Swedish bars in far-flung foreign cities even offer non-Swedes the chance to put flowers in their hair and join in the idyll from London to Tokyo.

In the town of Vimmerby, inland from the port of Väster-vik where the boats sail for Gotland and Almedalen in summertime, tourists and city-dwellers are gearing up for the main event. Vimmerby is like many small towns in the Swedish interior, a mish-mash of old wooden buildings joined by mid-century housing. The clipped lawns and quiet streets lead up to a town square with a council hall at one end and the local *Stadshotell*, or town hotel, at the other. It is a familiar layout in small towns across the country where local lodging houses sprang up for tired travelers in an age when people travelled slowly and had reasons to stay more than a few hours at a time.

Every so often a train calls at the spartan local railway station on its way to the coast, but there is no direct connec-tion to Stockholm and the wider world. It is one of many things that mean Vimmerby is in most ways unremarkable compared to any other town amongst the trees of contempo-rary Sweden; it has less industry than was previously the case and the fine dining is largely limited to the local pizzeria or the restaurant of the *Stadshotell*. Occasionally the local foot-ball team is promoted or relegated, or meets a big name team on a cup run. In Vimmerby the pizzeria just off of the main square is owned, like many across small town Sweden, by Balkan immigrants. Top of the menu is the Pizza Astrid, containing all of the ingredients available on the counter. This includes Béarnaise sauce and French fries in a heap, a show of excess hard to find elsewhere in rural and tradition-ally thrifty Småland.

The Pizza Astrid owes its name to the town's most famous daughter, Astrid Lindgren. Astrid herself is commemorated in bronze outside of the city hall, just down from the tourist office. Another statue elsewhere in the town was deemed too abstract by the local arbiters of taste, so outside the council

The Assembly Hall of the Riksdag, Sweden's Parliament.

Looking out from the Swedish Parliament towards Stockholm City Hall.

The Grand Hotel Saltsjöbaden, where the Saltsjöbad agreement was signed in 1938, making official the collective bargaining agreements which still define workers' rights in Sweden today.

Feminist debate at the Gothenburg Book Fair; a highlight of the social calendar for Sweden's chattering classes, and a chance for the country to market itself to the world at large.

Prime Minister Olof Palme addresses a crowd in Almedalen, Visby, in 1968.

Cinema grand where Olof Palme saw the movie *Bröderna Mozart* on the night of his assassination.

Crowds enjoying the Paradiset Restaurant at the 1930
Stockholm Exhibition.

The Stockholm exhibition from the air – the fair helped popularise the
modernist architectural ideals Sweden is famed for.

Prince Bertil of Sweden opening Skärholmen housing project in 1968, one of Sweden's successful planned postwar suburbs.

These days, like many suburbs built as part of the Million programme, Skärholmen is home largely to lower income families and immigrants.

Headquarters of the world's largest iron ore mine in Kiruna, Norrbotten.
The town is in the process of being moved, to avoid subsiding
into the mine below.

Eriksberg, a new suburb built on the ashes of shipbuilding
for Sweden's growing middle class.

Roma Migrants in Stockholm.

In the depths of the Stockholm Metro, often the best place for many Roma to find shelter whilst they try to earn money.

Scale model of Shanghai's 6.8 kilometre 'Swedish Town', which was built in 2004.

The completed Swedish Town; decidedly un-Swedish.

chambers a frozen Astrid sits at her desk with a typewriter like a mannequin in a museum.

The bestselling writer is synonymous with a particular view of Sweden, and at the peak of her fame Lindgren became the third most translated writer for young people in the world after Hans Christian Andersen and the Brothers Grimm, building a profitable global literary empire on the back of her pantheon of characters. The most famous in the English speaking countries was anarchic flame-haired troublemaker Pippi Longstocking, but from Japan to Germany she achieved fame and recognition over half a century of prolific writing. When she died in 2002 her coffin was driven through central Stockholm in a carriage, and she will soon be commemorated on new Swedish banknotes. For many people around the world, the small towns and green landscapes of Lindgren's work are their first encounter with Swedish imaginary.

On the edge of Vimmerby, at the end of a huge expanse of tarmac containing cars with Danish and German number plates, is another Sweden that does its best to meet these imagined expectations. Astrid Lindgren's World is a theme park, and the theme is unmistakably Sweden. Beyond the entrance gate is a replica of an old Swedish street, its bakeries, toyshops and cafes more lively than the real town centre down the road. Behind the high wire fence, the '50s hotdog stand and the petrol station are a hyper-real reconstruction of a small town Sweden from the popular imagination. Within a few hundred metres of each other are stereotypical farms, a Stockholm street, miniature replica houses and live animals to pet.

The storybook Sweden behind the fence of Astrid Lindgren's World is a meticulous reconstruction of the books of the giant of children's literature; the buildings are undersized so that children might look like adults, and the adults look like giants dressed in casual sweaters and sensible shoes. As you advance up through the park, the mild escapism of the 1950s sweet shops and bakeries gets more and more extreme, until you emerge at the castle of *Ronja the Robber's Daughter*, a Robin-Hood style adventure set deep in the forests of the Swedish North. A hundred yards away is the fake medieval square of *The Brothers Lionheart*, a tale of adventure in a mythical dream kingdom with strong hints of CS Lewis. In the latter, extras dressed as castle guards in chainmail stand around between performances. Periodically they try to frighten passing children as parents sip coffee under an ambivalent summer sky that shifts indecisively from grey to blue. Beyond the fiberglass stones of the fake castle and Ronja's woodland fortress lies another wire fence, where the fantasy fades once more into the neat rows of houses in a small town suburbs, less marketable than the condensed miniature Sweden available on the inside. The clipped lawns and postwar housing are more real but somehow less typical than the fantasy world they border.

There is, though, an irony to Vimmerby's hyper-Swedishness; the town has survived well compared to some of its counterparts elsewhere, and tourism provides a steady flow of income and jobs. All across the country in similar sized communities EU subsidies provide support for regions to reinvent themselves, trying to locate a uniquely marketable Swedishness that can be packaged and punted to city dwellers and foreign tourists alike. The hunt for a signature attraction and a local figure to elevate is a constant pursuit for regional politicians seeking to put their town back on the map. Sweden's urbanisation means that traditional small town life, once an important component in both the economy and the nation's identity, is playing less and less of a role in the national picture. Robbed of industry and inhabitants, it is easy to be forgotten in a country so sprawling.

Ironically, local authorities can both increase their population and make money by taking in asylum seekers and refugees. Thousands of Iraqis, Syrians and Somalians have found themselves transported to towns of small wooden houses and deep forests, heavy winter snow traditional identities upon arrival. Tellingly the Somalian national bandy team – a variation of hockey played on ice – is based in Borlänge, a steel town in the very centre of the players' adopted country.

Southwest of Vimmerby, over an almost continuous sweep of lakes and forests, lies the town of Växjö. Long before they put on suits and conquered Stockholm the Sweden Democrats were holding demonstrations in this part of the country, lining up with banners and black military jackets behind riot police to keep Sweden Swedish. This is Mattias Karlsson's home turf, and the region where the blue and yellow of the Sweden Democrat's populist surge began to make inroads. It was also here that one of the most iconic images of two competing ideas of Swedishness was created. On 13 April 1985 neo-Nazis clashed with members of the Swedish Left Party in the centre of town, and an opportunistic photographer captured a Polish-Swedish immigrant, Danuta Danielsson, hitting one of the Nazi marchers with her handbag. The pensioner was not a Left Party member but merely a passerby, and soon became an unlikely cult hero. Danielsson passed away in 1988, and three decades later an attempt was made to erect a statue of her wielding her handbag in Växjö, but it was overruled by local politicians on the grounds that it could promote violence. According to newspaper reports, other local authorities subsequently expressed an interest in putting themselves on the tourist map by taking the statue.

In 1994 the Sweden Democrats also held a rally in Växjo, on the cusp of their slow and painful transformation into a modern and socially acceptable movement. Party and supporters lined up with Swedish flags, shaved heads and black combat jackets; it was to be another two years before the organisation was forced to ban the wearing of military uniforms at its meetings. It was the same summer that a young dreadlocked Henrik Larsson hit the global stage at the World Cup in America as Sweden brought home a bronze medal. The Sweden squad was full of players with mixed ethnic backgrounds. The country was also about to vote the Social Democrats back into power, but even then it was clear that Sweden was changing. It was in this climate that Allan Pred, analyst of the Stockholm exhibition and the country's path in the modern world, wrote of Sweden's complex racial politics:

> Racisms are flourishing even in Sweden, a country long stereotyped by Western intellectuals and progressives as a paradise of social enlightenment, as an international champion of social justice.

Pred may well have written his appraisal of Sweden in the late 1990s, but his words are just as true today. In the bright clean future of the Swedish modern, Swedishness is still a problematic and contested element. For some people Zlatan will never be Swedish, yet for others he is a national icon.

Behind the locked gates of Astrid Lindgren's world there are no Roma sitting outside of the petrol station or concrete apartment blocks looming over the low wooden rows. The weather-boarded houses in the small woodland towns of Astrid Lindgren are an integral part of Swedish nationalism, but a banal nationalism which exists below the surface in contrast to the explicit nationalism of the far right, yet the two are still inextricably linked. Somewhat fittingly Hanna Zetterberg, the young girl who played Ronja the Robber's Daughter on TV and became a familiar face to millions of

Swedes and non-Swedes alike, would go on to sit in parliament for the Swedish Left Party after the 1994 election. As ever with Astrid Lindgren, just looking at the surface was not the whole story, and being a national icon is very different to being a nationalist.

The Sweden Democrats have attempted to annex Lindgren as part of the Swedish cultural canon, claiming *the Brothers Lionheart* embodied their core values, but Astrid Lindgren herself would disagree. When challenged about the portrayal of Swedes and non-Swedes in her books, Lindgren replied:

> It was hard and bitter to hear for someone who despises all nationalism as innately as I do. I thought you would know that. I thought you knew, that I dislike all division of people into nations and races, all sorts of discrimination between white and black, Aryan and Jews, between Turks and Swedes, between men and women. Since I was tall enough to think for myself I have disliked the blue and yellow motherland ideal of Sweden...

To achieve certain things you need a sense of community, Olof Palme told David Frost in 1969, but that community need not exclude others. Sweden for the Swedes could well be a positive rallying cry if, indeed, anyone can be Swedish. Back in Stockholm the national football team's star player is immortalised with his Volvo estate car in front of an icy landscape on the advertising hoardings of the metro. It may well be a case of Sweden for the Swedes, but whatever Mattias Karlsson thinks, Zlatan is more Swedish than almost anything else.

The material that makes up this chapter was only written eight months before publication, but since then Sweden has been shaken to its core by the political implications of the Syrian refugee crisis. A preoccupation with Roma migrants was dwarfed by the arrival of large numbers of Syrians escaping conflict, further pressuring the Swedish government.

In the autumn of 2015 the Swedish Deputy Prime Minister Åsa Romson burst into tears at a government press conference as she unveiled changes to Swedish refugee policy. In just a few months, Sweden took in the most refugees per capita of any country in Western Europe. This pales into insignificance compared to the refugee Syrian populations of Turkey and Lebanon, but still placed Sweden well ahead of its Nordic and European neighbours. Suddenly, Syrian families clutching suitcases became a familiar sight at Swedish railway stations. Sweden reintroduced border checks for the first time since 1995 to try and regulate the migration into the country, ramping up the severity bit by bit in response to political pressure.

The Sweden Democrats could not believe their luck. After years of complaining that Sweden was on the cusp of takeover by Islamic migrants, television channels and newspapers were filled with images of a government struggling to cope with the challenge of such a rise in asylum applications.

They issued a statement demanding Sweden immediately stop all new asylum applications and leave the European Union. Sweden, they claimed, was full. By offering asylum to those fleeing war, Sweden was contributing to the crisis and forcing migrants to take risks, they claimed.

In Trollhättan near Gothenburg a 21-year old with far-right sympathies walked into a school and killed three people, targeting anyone with non-European ethnic backgrounds. Hate crime in Sweden reached new highs and there was political deadlock over what to do.

Trying to read the public mood, the Social Democrats rediscovered some of their former enthusiasm for a closed welfare model and began to talk more openly about properly allocating resources and what a country like Sweden could realistically do. The Sweden Democrats had hit 20 per cent in the polls. There was a string of arson attacks and vandalism against temporary housing allocated to asylum seekers.

The Social Democrats sought legal permission to close the Öresund bridge between Denmark and Sweden for up to a month at a time if the necessity arose. Sweden, so long a poster-child for refugee policy, had changed fundamentally. It had tried to do the right thing, but ultimately its hands were tied.

In the January of 2016 the government announced that it was looking to potentially remove tens of thousands of asylum seekers back to their countries of origin. Many others are now subject to temporary residency laws. Even in Sweden, politics bites.

CHAPTER SIX

Ecotopia

A sustainable country in a dirty world

*Our dream was a dream for those who wander
from the graveled cities*

ELIN WÄGNER

IT IS SEPTEMBER 2014, just a few days after Sweden's general elections, and the exact makeup of the country's new government is still uncertain. In a shopping centre in the heart of Stockholm people stream in from the street and drink coffee at espresso bars in the atrium between the stores.

In a gap between the coffee and smoothie stands is a small stage, and on it two people with microphones are talking to nobody in particular. Maria Wetterstrand is the former co-leader of the Swedish Green Party, and next to her is Gabriel Liljenström, an environmental activist who will go on to work on the country's new Green-led development team. A small crowd of onlookers gathers round to hear Wetterstrand speak as she and Liljenström unveil their new book, *What is environment?*

It is an odd setting for two people committed to a completely sustainable society to be looking for their public, but in Sweden being green is all a part of being seen. As the crowds disperse, Liljenström climbs down from the stage and pulls up one of the stools meant to entice tired shoppers into the audience. In a smart blazer and a bow tie he is a particularly presentable face for the environmental movement.

'The environment is quite mainstream in Sweden,' says

Liljenström. 'All the parties try and profile themselves as green. In that sense we have achieved a breakthrough for the environment, and the environment is a big issue for Swedes.'

Judging by appearance at least, Sweden is a global leader in combatting environmental problems. It was the first state in the world to establish an environmental protection agency, and just down the street from where Wetterstrand and Liljenström have been talking the UN organised the first conference on global environment in 1972. Since then though the world has changed as Sweden tries to balance sustainability with guaranteeing the wealth people have become accustomed to.

'It always features in the top three concerns in polls, but then Swedes have an outdated picture of themselves,' Liljenström says. 'We were among the most progressive countries in the world in the '90s, but today we're on the climate blacklist. Sometimes if you criticise our environmental record people think you are trying to talk the country down.'

After the inconclusive election, Wetterstrand and Liljenström's party have just been able to forge a deal with the Social Democrats. It is a deal that means Stefan Löfven, a former welder with links to the metalworkers union, finds himself making a speech in which the environment plays a rhetorically prominent role. Rising from the ashes of the 1980s anti-nuclear movement, the Greens have spent the last decade readying themselves for government, and now find themselves a powerful voice as junior partners to Löfven's Social Democrats. It has not been an easy journey; like many Green movements they began by promising to redraw politics as people knew it, but the public disagreed. From the mid-1990s onwards they began to find a more natural home on the traditional political spectrum, nestling between the Socialist parties and the political centre without ever fully signing up to either.

From his office window on Stockholm's South Island, Green Party chairman Anders Wallner can see the Swedish parliament across the weir where the freshwater of Sweden's inland lakes meets the Baltic Sea. Wallner himself is typical of the new face of Green politics in Sweden, youthful, easygoing and concerned with social exclusion and human rights as much as the environment. He has attempted to profile the party as a young and dynamic alternative to the older, more dogmatic politics of the Social Democrats and Left Party, pushing a vision of a socially liberal and environmentally responsible progressive society. As the only party sceptical about the advantages of boundless economic growth that underpins the Swedish model, it is a tough sell. When Gösta Rehn and Rudolf Meidner came up with their plan for the Swedish economy in the technological optimism of the 1950s, nobody had really considered that it could lead to environmental crisis half a century down the line.

'You can see we now have a chance to introduce more of a Green angle to government and then hopefully grow in light of what we will be able to show has changed,' Wallner says optimistically. 'We have also opened up the discussion toward big investments in rail and public transport, completely renewable energy and more funding for biodiversity.'

Biodiversity may be important, but the railways are more of a sore point for most Swedes. Semi-privatised in the early 1990s, each winter brings chaos as infrastructure fails in freezing temperatures, whilst Stockholm's central station is regularly bought to a standstill. Outside of Wallner's office window runs Sweden's main north-south rail line, and when it is out of action the Stockholm region falls apart.

In environmental terms though, the enduring problem for contemporary Sweden is that it suffers from being one of Europe's most consumer driven societies. A recent ranking by the WWF placed Sweden just behind the US and Gulf states in terms of its global environmental impact. The nation's wealth has created an insatiable appetite for consumer goods, meat and long distance travel. Less affected by the global economic downturn than the Eurozone or the UK, it has carried on spending in the globalised marketplace. Its middle class regularly winter in the Far East and central Stockholm is filled with large jeeps and estate cars belonging to its wealthy suburban commuters.

With its seemingly endless forests and pristine lake systems though, Sweden is also a paradise for people wishing to escape the big cities and live the green dream, yet 30 years on from the Stockholm conference, the impacts of environmental degradation are still clearly visible in Sweden, from the bare hillsides of industrial forestry to increasing urban sprawl. The phenomenal pace of urbanisation means that planning things properly is an obstacle to providing homes and coping with changing populations. Neither is the country safe from the impacts of extreme weather; two years ago a forest fire tore through the region of Västmanland west of Stockholm, forcing people from their homes. The outgoing government was generally perceived to have responded badly, and an inquiry was launched to improve the country's resilience to climate change and natural disasters.

On an international level, Swedish governments past and present have been keen to show their green credentials in diplomatic circles. At the largely inconclusive Copenhagen climate summit in 2009 Sweden joined its Scandinavian neighbours in marketing something called 'The Nordic Way', a green version of the Scandinavian model that claimed to have solved welfare and inequality alongside guaranteeing environmental sustainability and third world development. Unfortunately for Nordic moral sensibilities, the American

Way and the Chinese Way proved to hold more sway. Christine Ingebritsen, a researcher at the University of Washington in the US, has referred to Scandinavia as a 'moral superpower' in the way it tries to portray itself around the world, and at home to the environment is an easy way to feel good, and being green is increasingly part of the Scandinavian catalogue lifestyle.

* * *

One place where you can live the green dream is the new Stockholm district of Hammarby Sjöstad. Across the canal from Stockholm's hip Södermalm Island its location is marked by the smoke plume of a plant producing energy from waste and a huge artificial ski slope burning fluorescent in the winter darkness. Reachable by tram or bike from the city, the district heating keeps the homes warm and the long planted boulevards keep it looking green. Facing the flowing water, Hammarby Sjöstad is a shining example of Sweden's rhetorical mainstreaming of environmentalism. It was built at the turn of the millennium on former industrial land, replacing abandoned factory units and a shantytown out of keeping with the clean lines and aspirations of the modern city. With its quayside apartments, reed beds, water features and jetties it offers its residents a high quality of life in a setting in which being green need not inconvenience them.

At its centre lies the old Luma lightbulb factory, a towering masterpiece of functional open rooms and clean edges rising high above the old dockside. When Marquis Childs came to Sweden in the '30s he picked the factory out as an exportable example of both Swedish architecture and cooperative business. Today it is an office complex with an attached microbrewery and restaurant selling food made from fresh domestically sourced ingredients. The Luma factory's functional modernist lines fit seamlessly with the reborn Hammarby Sjöstad lifestyle. A one-room flat could cost you upwards of two million kronor, but it is clean and green for those with money to spend. The official brochure for the Hammarby Sjöstad project goes into great detail about its pioneering traits – Sustainable building materials in its buildings, non-toxic paints on the cycle bridges that will not pollute the local water courses when it snows, heat and hot water generated from waste, all part of a self-declared 'Hammarby Model'. Hammarby Sjöstad invites its occupants to a future not so much sustainable as smug.

On the main street through the district is a branch of the iconic Swedish hamburger chain MAX. On a Thursday in late February it is *sportlov* in Stockholm – a time when people generally leave the city for winter sports breaks in the country – and people are queueing at the self-service machines in MAX Hammarby Sjöstad. Children off school but stuck in the city munch on French fries as their parents stare at the grey skies out of the window. Every so often one of the trams built to serve the new eco-town swings around the corner down the long planted avenues. Started by an entrepreneur in northern Sweden in the late 1960s, MAX is ubiquitous as McDonalds in the country. Their branches fill retail units in shopping centres and airports, railway stations and retail parks from Sweden's southern tip to its Arctic north.

Selling themselves on their Swedishness, MAX are engaged in a constant war with McDonalds for market share, and part of the chain's strategy is their environmental record. Their hamburgers are climate neutral thanks to a tree-planting scheme in Uganda, and on the menus behind the teenagers who pack meat into buns each meal carries a carbon label. You can even gorge ethically on a Green Meal for 69 kronor.

Directed at vegans and the environmentally conscious, customers can eat sustainably among the wipe-clean surfaces and generic landscape photos on the wall. The company's motto is 'a sustainable MAX in a sustainable society', and they have won international prizes for their idiosyncratic fusion of Scandinavian environmental awareness and American fast food capitalism.

MAX, though, is just one part of Hammarby Sjöstad's green continuation of the norm. Down the street from the plate glass windows of the restaurant is an Audi dealership, reached by passing the entrance to one of the huge road tunnels that sweep invisibly under Stockholm's inner suburbs. In 2014 the residents of Hammarby Sjöstad voted overwhelmingly for the Moderates over any other party, with the Greens in third place and the Centre party even further behind. The Moderates have been keen to push a lifetstyle-based big city environmentalism to their supporters, with the conflict between sustainability and living the green dream buried out of sight in concrete-lined motorway tunnels and Asian factories. According to the Stockholm Environment Institute, Sweden's emissions are 17 per cent higher when the impact of its consumer behaviour overseas is factored in. The country's immense wealth creates phenomenal consumer demand, and there is now a direct container route run by Danish shipping giant Maersk from Gothenburg to Hong Kong, Shanghai, Korea and Japan to keep Sweden in a ready supply of computers, phones, televisions and electronics.

This normalisation of an environmentally friendly everyday embodied by Hammarby Sjöstad is part of a much wider process that has taken place in Swedish society over the past two decades. In the 1990s the country went through a period of what academics have called 'ecological modernisation'. This meant that as economic shocks and a changing economy marked the end of one period in Swedish economic history, being green became a way to embrace a new future. In 1996 the Swedish Prime Minister, Göran Persson, made a speech in which he envisioned the creation of a 'green people's home', an updated version of the old Social Democratic metaphor in which sustainability was a key part of the country and the future.

Robyn Eckersley, an Australian political scientist and leading thinker on sustainability has even lauded Sweden as an example of what a 'green state' might look like – a country which has moved toward complete sustainability. The enduring problem for Sweden is that it is part of a global economy. Fittingly, Sweden's problems with the wider world are best found far from its capital, in the woods and pristine wilderness of the High North and the snows of the Arctic Circle.

* * *

'If you want a cheap kitchen fan or some radiators get in there,' chuckles Kjell Törmä, editor of the local newspaper in the Swedish city of Kiruna, tucked away in Norrbotten at the very top of Sweden. Sat behind the wheel of his well-heated car, he points at the red-brick apartment blocks on the edge of his hometown, high above the Arctic Circle in splendid isolation. The red blocks are part of Ullspiran, a district of municipal housing that is about to become the first victim of Kiruna's hollow earth and a resource-hungry global economy. 2015 marked a turning point for the residents of Sweden's northernmost city. With the melting of the heavy winter snows, the bulldozers moved in to make way for expansion of its lifeblood; a huge iron ore mine that winds over a kilometre underground on the other side of the valley and is eating Kiruna from below.

The city sits on a gargantuan seam of high grade magnetite, an iron ore that has kept the Arctic economy ticking over for more than a century. When extraction first started in 1898 the tops were taken off two local hills, Kirunavaara and Luossavaara, and huge clefts were cut into them along the seam. When the ore was all gone the miners continued underground, moving ever closer to the town. Today the seam of magnetite is mined deeper than ever, and with each trainload of ore that finds its way to foreign markets the existence of the city becomes ever more precarious. Kiruna is being forced to relocate a few miles down the road; a new town to last another hundred years, or until the ore runs out.

In 2013 Swedish state owned mining company LKAB made a profit of 700 million dollars from its Arctic mines, though in reality the income is higher as the state pays tax to itself. The huge profits help to keep Sweden's schools and hospitals running and the north of the country alive. The sheer amount of money which the mine can provide means that there was never any question of closing it and letting the city remain. Back in his office, sipping syrupy black coffee that has been cooking for hours on the stove, Törmä describes his work documenting the end of one Kiruna and the birth of another.

'In 2004 LKAB produced their first estimations, and then a lot of people said "Nothing is happening." There's been a lot of preparation, and then infrastructure work such as the new railway and power system. Now though you'll begin to see it properly as they tear the old town down and they start building.' The project means it is year zero for a cleaner, greener and altogether more hospitable reinvention of the frontier city. Törmä's *Kiruna Tidning* has a strong civic pride. Most newspapers in Sweden have a political leaning, but in Kiruna the stated allegiance on the banner is 'local patriotic'.

'Our distribution area runs from Sao Paulo northwards,' jokes Törmä wryly. 'We've one person in Brazil we've had since the beginning. About half of the subscribers live elsewhere.

We've lost so many people over the years – there were 34,000 of us at one point, but now we're just 23,000.' Kiruna's story is a familiar one across Scandinavian, as changing economics and mechanisation have meant fewer jobs in heavy industry; it is always at the mercy of global markets.

'At the end of the '70s and beginning of the '80s LKAB landed itself in a deep crisis. I left school in 1978 and there were 26 of us from that class. A year later it was just me and one other person left in town.' says Törmä.

'In the '70s and the early '80s people were just leaving – the mine could have gone under and the state was forced to come in and take over. Then there was an upturn, and the last 15 years have seen huge growth – to the point there is now a housing shortage.'

From the car park outside the newspaper office the mine is visible across the valley, as is the crumbling and cracked empty ground above the current mine workings. The rate of extraction from the Kiruna mine is breathtaking; around the clock the most powerful electric rail locomotives in the world pull trains of iron ore across the border to Norway and the Atlantic Ocean for export to China, the Middle East and the US. LKAB has transformed the whole of the North of Sweden into a single technological megasystem, and it is the global demand for steel products that keeps Kiruna going. One of the main customers is Bahrain, but LKAB's products also find their way to China, North America and Germany. The mine and its cluster of processing plants hums away under the midnight sun and in the winter darkness atop its decapitated mountain. Wherever you are in Kiruna the mine is always present. Like the living planet in Stanislaw Lem's *Solaris* it stares back into the lives of those in its orbit, people who came to exploit the earth but have now found the mine has the upper hand over them.

Eventually Törmä's office and every other building in central Kiruna will vanish into an expanding sinkhole that is already biting at the city limits. As the mine digs deeper into the ore seam, cracks are inching across what was once a lakebed, now a sealed off zone of scrub and unstable black spoil speckled with snow. The railway line that once ran between the city and the mine has been relocated, arching around the back of the Kirunavaara hill between frozen ponds of tailings – the dirty waste runoff from mine operations once the ore has been extracted.

On the other side of the city the first signs of the new Kiruna are emerging from firmer ground. A few miles east and out of the bite of the cold arctic wind a large sign stands by the roadside proclaiming the construction of the new settlement. Deer tracks and the imprints of snowmobile tread mark the soft snow, too weak to walk on but too deep to walk through. Over the next decade the empty woodland around the sign will be transformed into a model community of the future, all designed by the world-renowned White Architects from Stockholm, 14 hours south by sleeper train.

In 2014 the municipality signed a deal with LKAB for 3.74 billion kronor, around 375 million dollars, to build much of what will replace the current downtown area. Elements of the architects' vision for a new Kiruna are straight from a science fiction novel, including a 10km long cable car that will lift passengers above the trees and winter snows, transporting them from the airport to the local railway station and the huge ore mine. Temperatures in the winter can regularly dip below minus 30, and the new city will be triple glazed and 'climate smart' according to its glowing press release.

In the Arctic it stays completely dark for a few weeks each year, as the sun never rises, so the new town is also intended to be a light and sociable place. At the centre of this modern marvel will be the new city hall, The Crystal, with public rooms and bright white lights to beat the winter blues. It will make Kiruna into one of the most efficient, modern and environmentally friendly cities in Europe. Kiruna's current city hall, a masterpiece of open 1960s functionalism by the architect Artur von Schmalensee, acts as an indoor public square for the city's residents in the coldest months of the year. The new building is designed to achieve a similar function, and though von Schmalensee's creation will be reduced to rubble, the distinctive metal clock tower will be saved and planted in the heart of the new Kiruna as a nod to the past.

In Kiruna's only bookshop, right in the heart of the old city, 22-year-old Jessica Wennberg sits behind the counter counting the receipts. The building is a typical slice of 1950s Sweden with its elegantly lettered sign and stacks of stationery in the display window. Another Kiruna native, she came back to the city after attending music college further south.

'I like it here. There's a lot to do and the nature is wonderful,' she ponders. The low brick building housing the business will be another casualty of the move though. 'We don't know how long we'll be here, but everyone will get a new premises... coming back was not a hard decision, and the business is doing alright,' she says with an optimistic smile.

Another key element of Kiruna's sustainable masterplan is that no home should be more than three blocks from the city centre, or three blocks from the Arctic woodland surrounding it on all sides. The wilderness that envelopes Kiruna is the least densely populated area in Western Europe. If you leave the town passing northwards you will not see as much as a road before crossing into Norway on the way to the Arctic Ocean. This wilderness, blue and white in winter and shades of green and brown in summer, attracts tourists from all over the world to bask in its emptiness and see the local indigenous Sami culture.

Just outside of Kiruna lies the village of Jukkesjärvi, famous for its tourist-attracting Ice Hotel. Direct flights from London and elsewhere mean that people can fly into Kiruna and meet Father Christmas, stay in the ice hotel and be taken on guided walks of the winter wonderland without ever entering the metropolitan Sweden far to the south. On a tourist route of Sami villages, winter sports and champagne in the Ice Hotel, it is a small slice of the continent as packaged as central Paris or the Scottish Highlands. The local tourist office markets the region not as Norrbotten but as 'Swedish Lapland'.

It is a source of local pride, but this winter wonderland that attracts tourists year on year, is melting. Climate change means that in the hundred years in which mine will move down, the air temperature will rise. In the next half-century models predict that Kiruna will see a three-degree rise in temperature. If there is no change in the global output of greenhouse gases it could be higher still. Isolated, Kiruna is in a Faustian pact with the industrialised world outside, selling its mineral wealth and its culture in return for being allowed to exist. Yet, half a mile underground, Maja Landström is enthusiastic about the new city. Dressed in a hard hat and the branded LKAB overalls, she leads visitors along abandoned mineshafts on a tour of the huge facility. In her 50s and from the area, she moved back to Kiruna from Stockholm with her family, attracted by a better quality of life.

'The mine is the most important thing in Kiruna,' she says. 'Without the mine there would be no city, almost everyone has some kind of connection to it... I'm born in Kiruna and there's always been talk of moving the city. My hometown is vanishing and my memories will go with it, but it will be a better city environment.'

Landström's mixed emotions are at the heart of the trade off the town is making with its own history. The new city will try and preserve some of the past by moving a few signature buildings, including the old wooden church dating from when Kiruna was an inhospitable frontier outpost.

'They're going to take care of some of the older stuff and try and mix it. I think most people are positive to it and think it is going to be a big improvement. I'm happy that LKAB exists and that they are here to stay,' she says optimistically.

The truth of the matter is that job security is still good in Kiruna compared to other parts of rural Sweden. Wages are high too, even by Swedish standards. Mineworkers can earn around 2,600 pounds a month after tax plus bonuses by working shifts, and there is at least 100 years of ore left. In contrast a privately run mine in Pajala, a few hundred miles to the east, recently closed when the company that owned it collapsed. Mineral speculation is a fragile business, and dependent on the whim of the global economy. In the official LKAB narrative though the future has no victims.

Visitors to the Kiruna mine are given a tiny bag of pellets – the small balls of ore that most buyers want – as a souvenir. LKAB is particularly proud that its iron ore is more environmentally friendly than its competitors, and its magnetite is marketed under the rubric of 'green pellets'. In the information displays of the LKAB facility one of the pellets is visually represented as a seed with a small green shoot growing out of it, surrounded by pictures of smiling, healthy and environmentally conscious workers. During earth hour – the worldwide simultaneous switching off of lights to save energy – LKAB issued a press release that boasted 'we celebrate earth hour every day' in a cheery attempt to show how heavy industry and saving the planet can co-exist. Each year the company uses over 20 gigawatt hours of electricity, equivalent to around two per cent of Sweden's total consumption. In the LKAB promotional film played to visitors this emphasis on sustainability builds to a crescendo as helicopter shots of the Arctic landscape are mixed with a voiceover and ambiguously ethnic music. The narrator explain how the source of both Kiruna's prosperity and the developing world's sustainability emerges from the untainted and pure Norrbotten earth. It looks and feels like an advert for mineral water, presenting iron ore as a lifestyle product for the ethically aware.

Not everyone is happy about the way the mining company dictates the city's future. Henry Emmeroth, a local Green councillor and environmentalist, says that the state-owned empire expects the city to simply do as it is told.

'The Swedish state is only interested in the huge profits LKAB has made for the national coffers for decades. They blast in the mine until two in the morning so you cannot sleep. They release heavy metals and other dangerous chemicals like mercury, meaning Kiruna has the most polluted lake in Sweden, a stone's throw from the city centre. Our cultural inheritance, our history and our pride is being torn apart. Traders in the centre of town, homeowners and people renting have no idea what their future is,' Emmeroth complains. 'Older people cannot afford to move into new homes with higher rents. They have to leave Kiruna, and these are the same people who helped build the city when times were hard.' The alternative, though, is Kiruna ceasing to exist altogether.

Kiruna is an extreme case of the problems afflicting Norrland, the collective name for almost half of the Sweden that begins a few hours north of Stockholm at the Dalaälv River. Norrland is an extraction economy, irrespective of what is being mined, farmed or felled. When other European countries were busy colonising Africa, Asia and the Americas to reap their natural resources Sweden colonised itself. Axel Oxenstierna, a Swedish nobleman and royal adviser in the 17th century declared 'In Norrland we have our own India.' A few hundred years later it was declared that Norrland was Sweden's own American west.

Few people in modern times have done more to challenge this than Sara Lidman, a radical novelist and journalist from a small community inland of the Norrlandic high coast who became a champion of the Swedish north in her writings and activism. Lidman was an uncompromising opponent of the environmental degradation and brutal economics that characterised Sweden's own colony. Lidman turned the idea of the people's home on its head, pointing to the regional inequalities – linguistic, cultural and economic – that contradicted the picture of a homogenous happy national family. In 1968 she released a book about the Kiruna mine, a picture which the government in Stockholm claimed was wholly false. The following year workers in the northern Swedish mines engaged in wildcat strikes, bringing the Arctic's technological megasystem to a standstill. For Lidman it was like a colonial uprising.

Today the issues are still there – timber and minerals leave, and so do people. On a concrete overbridge by Kiruna's abandoned and soon to be swallowed railway station someone has sprayed 'This is not Sweden – Autonomous Norrbotten' on the retaining wall. The transplantation of Kiruna is not at an easy process, and the planners have been tasked not just with building a new residential district but with recreating the old Kiruna in a new form. That means finding a corresponding place for everything the town currently has, including its complex culture and politics, and its contradictions.

Alongside Jessica Wennberg's bookshop there will be a new high street with all the familiar names and big Swedish brands like H&M, ensuring another hundred years of consumer comfort for those selling the Norrlandic earth. Up the street from the bookshop, in the window of a local architect's office, a sign boasts 'Kiruna is like Detroit'. The American city has become a byword for post-industrial landscapes at the end of the American century, but Kiruna wants to carry on living. To do so it needs the dirty world around it to buy its environmentally-friendly Swedish ore.

* * *

In the 1930s, as Gunnar Asplund was planning a bright new world of industrial prosperity and Social Democratic politicians dreamed of an efficient society of industry and modern model people, another less famous Swede was plotting a different path. Years before her time, Elin Wägner was a pioneering feminist and ecological thinker who largely vanished under the weight of the Swedish modern after the Second World War. A green utopian, her warnings of the perils of limitless growth went unheeded in the technological optimism of the '50s and '60s, a time of motorways and nuclear power stations, mass manufacturing and industrial forestry. Unfortunately for Wägner, Sweden is a place in which the modern always wins out.

Now, although the country has great ambitions both to be green and to be seen as green the big question of whether it can transition to real sustainability and become a genuinely green state is still unanswered and will probably remain so for some time. Sweden has Greens in government and seemingly genuine will to make significant improvements to the sustainability of the country, but is also caught in a conflict with its own near past and the constant need to grow its economy.

Jonas Hinnfors is a Professor of Political Science at

Gothenburg University and a close watcher of the Swedish Social Democrats.

'I think it will be hard for the Greens to make any impact at all in terms of getting away from the growth economy,' he says of Sweden's Green dawn. 'It will be in the details that they will no doubt be able to make a difference, and that means they can use it as a symbolic marker that the party is on the way to changing people's views on growth.'

In Jukkesjärvi the ice is melting, and on the Arabian peninsula steel skyscrapers are being raised from the desert using LKAB's green pellets. Maersk container ships dock in Gothenburg with smartphones destined for Stockholm shopping arcades and flat screen TVs destined for eco-friendly apartments in prime waterfront locations. At the heart of Sweden's green people's home is a dilemma; If the Swedish model is to be made sustainable enough to last, it means voters being prepared to abandon some of the consumer prosperity they have grown used to. Even if Sweden's Green-tinged government can put the country at the forefront of global environmentalism once again, they are by no means out of the woods yet.

CHAPTER SEVEN

Cultural Utopia

How Sweden became a cultural powerhouse

Culture should be a dynamic, challenging and independent force with freedom of expression at its root.

OFFICAL STATEMENT OF THE SWEDISH PARLIAMENT

IN LATE MARCH as the last of the winter snow whipped around Stockholm and clung to the shadows. *Svenska Dagbladet*, one of Sweden's biggest newspapers, had a new headline at the top of its website: The Nobel Prize-winning poet Tomas Tranströmer is dead.

Every year the world waits with baited breath for the permanent secretary of the Swedish Academy to emerge from behind a set of close doors and announce the Nobel Prize in literature. The country that invented the award has given it to its own writers a few times over the last century, but Tranströmer was a writer considered a heavyweight well beyond Sweden's borders. His metaphysical poems drew worldwide acclaim, even if commercial success was not always forthcoming. Robbed of his ability to speak by a stroke, Tranströmer spent his final years with the written word as his only medium of communication, yet his voice remained.

Over 700 miles and two countries away, Sweden's Minister for Culture and Democracy was touching down in a state struggling desperately to maintain either. Rocked by civil war, saddled with a stagnant economy that can barely pay its military bills and with an uncertain future, Ukraine is another Europe, far from the literary prizes and cultural supplements of the Nordic countries but filling the front pages and TV channels across the world. In 2012 Ukraine met Sweden in the European Championship football finals. In the days running up to the match, Swedes posted pictures online of themselves drinking in the hot Ukrainian summer with their local opponents, both dressed in shades of yellow and blue and briefly a part of a unified and relatively peaceful continent. An impressive Zlatan Ibrahimovic had put one past the Ukrainians before the hosts came back to win in a party atmosphere. By the spring of 2015 though, the glittering Donbass Arena in the eastern city of Donetsk, where both teams played their fixtures, had been reduced to rubble in many places. Its plate glass windows were broken by shell fire and its pitch was unplayable.

As the Swedish delegation landed there were rumblings from America about military aid for the Ukrainian government, and the foreign offices of Western Europe were busy trying to come up with a solution to the growing crisis on their eastern border. In Sweden, however, their chosen envoy was not a tough talking diplomat but a half-Gambian former television presenter flanked by a crowd of culture experts. Neither were Alice Bah Kuhnke and her small team there to discuss the political situation, or at least not directly. Settling into their seats at the Ukrainian National Academy of music, the visitors had come to attend a performance of a documentary play about women's rights. Produced by a Swede in cooperation with the Swedish National Theatre and the brainchild of Swedish dramatist Hedda Krausz Sjögren, Kiev was one stop on a tour that would take the play to Belarus and Egypt among other places. Formed of seven monologues on the struggle for human rights it was a particularly Swedish type of soft power.

The Swedish delegation lamented the ongoing conflict and their Ukrainian hosts lamented the death of the poet Tranströmer. Ukraine is four times the size of Sweden, but it barely makes a dent in the global popular consciousness in comparison. After the performance there followed meeting after meeting with different cultural and political representatives, journalists, playwrights and activists. At the heart of Sweden's cultural diplomacy is a belief that culture can be a force for good. During the cold war Sweden acted as a bridge between east and west, and since the early '90s it has put huge diplomatic resources into rebuilding and fostering democracy in former Eastern Bloc states. To a cynic, dispatching a cultural delegation into the midst of a civil war might sound like fiddling as Rome burns, but Bah Kuhnke's trip to Ukraine reveals a lot about how instrumentally Sweden uses its cultural profile.

Cultural politics is serious business in Sweden and the public *kulturdebatt*, or cultural debate, is an important piece of Sweden's political puzzle. Picked from outside of politics to become a minister by the Greens, Bah Kuhnke is a skilled cultural diplomat, balancing a modern multicultural society and Sweden's sizeable cultural inheritance.

Sweden has long used its disproportionate cultural weight as a means of profiling itself around the world. Weeks before he met David Frost, worldwide cinema audiences had the chance to see Olof Palme in *I Am Curious (Yellow)*, a risqué new-wave project which liberally mixed fiction and reality to make a political point. The film was a globally successful exploration of class and sexuality, notable for including a discussion with Palme and his family on class society, as well as an interview with Martin Luther King and vox pops with normal working Swedes. Sat outside his house in the suburb of Vällingby, Palme's family pop up in shot and his children run around as he delivers a characteristically considered response to the questions posed. It became an international hit, in part due to its taboo-breaking depictions of casual sex, joining a long line of Swedish films to have made a world-wide impact.

In *I Am Curious (Yellow)* lead actress Lena Nyman spends large parts of the film with a radio microphone interviewing people on the street about the direction of Swedish society, asking them if the model people's home really was equal and what they planned to do about it. It was an unambiguously political film, but the cinema has long functioned as a more subtle means of both analysing Sweden and strengthening ideas about the country overseas. The Swedish Film Institute, a state-funded foundation, pumps tens of millions of kronor into film production each year. Sweden now kicks out around 30 feature films every 12 months, many of them generously supported by state grants to aid production. It has led to Sweden becoming a small but significant player in postwar cinema, providing talent to Hollywood but also producing an impressive output of domestically made films that win global acclaim.

A few weeks after touching down in Ukraine the Swedish Culture Minister was in the air again, this time on the way to the Cannes Film Festival. She was there to help unveil a documentary about Ingrid Bergman, the Swedish leading woman of *Casablanca* who became a Hollywood superstar in the 1930s and worked with Alfred Hitchcock, Roberto Rossellini and Ingmar Bergman among other stellar names. On the red carpet on the French Riviera the Swedish delegation was joined by Alicia Vikander, the latest Swede made good in Hollywood, and Isabela Rossellini, director and daughter of Bergman and Roberto. Sweden's cultural reach is great, and there is much to be gained from a profile as a creative powerhouse, keeping the world curious about the little country at the top of Europe and giving a profile about and beyond what its size might merit.

* * *

Film is not the only medium where Swedish culture has had a worldwide impact. It is a Friday night at Debaser Strand, a club on Södermalm in Stockholm that sits tucked into the shadow of one of the huge bridges that link the capital's disparate parts. Södermalm is the fashionable and trendy heart of the Swedish capital's arts and social scene, with ambitions to be mentioned in the same breath as Brooklyn in New York, Kreuzberg in Berlin or Shoreditch in East London. Tonight there are three indiepop bands taking to the stage.

The headliners are Alvvays, Canadian but marketed as sounding like Teenage Fanclub, Belle and Sebastian and Camera Obscura. By the strange process that countries pigeonhole one another, Scottish indie music is held in high esteem in the Swedish capital. On the wall of the club framed portraits of Bobby Gillespie from Primal Scream and Belle and Sebastian's Stuart Murdoch vie for space with Swedish names like First Aid Kit and Nina Persson from The Cardigans. First Aid Kit have just been rewarded for their international success with a special set of stamps by the Swedish Post Office, as has homemade Nordic pop icon Robyn. Sweden is the third biggest exporter of music in the world after the US and the United Kingdom, and the list of successful artists is seemingly endless.

At Debaser, named for a song by Pixies, the crowd are mostly veterans of the indie pop wave that swept the country in the early 2000s. In the half dark of the auditorium they wear T-shirts with the names of its luminaries; The Radio Dept, Sambassadeur, Vapnet and Jens Lekman. At the bar stands a tousle-haired follower of the Stockholm indie scene in a hoody and yet another band T-shirt.

'I don't know how Sweden got so good at music,' says Jonas Artursson as he sips fizzy lager, there with his girlfriend to watch the bands. 'It definitely was not always like this. It was only really in the '90s that things started to change.'

'What Sweden has is a really good garage band culture,' Artursson says. 'It felt like seemingly everybody has been in a band at some point and a lot of the stuff you see comes out of that. People change bands and get to know each other.'

Many of Sweden's musical stars first learn their trade in publicly funded music colleges, and the country is small enough to quickly develop contacts. In Swedish indie music it is easy to join the dots between the rotating members of different groups. A poster on the wall of Debaser Strand profiles an upcoming show by Nord och Syd, Sweden's hippest band according to the newspaper *Metro*, made up of members of several different groups from the last decade, now combined into an indie super-group pedaling home-made, fuzzy but melodic shoegaze.

In addition to its impressive indie output, Sweden also exports metal, house music and the inheritors of an independent jazz scene that blossomed in '50s Stockholm. Worldwide, Swedish songwriters and producers are often an invisible hand guiding successful musicians – it is not uncommon for smaller nations in the Eurovision song contest to buy-in Swedish mercenaries to write their entries. Exporting arts makes Sweden money, and money makes arts.

* * *

Another key element of the Swedish cultural powerhouse is its literature export market. On a Thursday morning in late September people dodge the drizzle and trams to reach the entrance of the Swedish Exhibition and Congress Centre in Gothenburg. They have come for the Gothenburg book fair, the largest in Northern Europe and the reason there are no hotel rooms to be had across the entire city.

The particularly Swedish iteration of the globally stand-ardised expo hall is an outdated idea of modern glamour, attached to a skyscraper with a fine dining restaurant at the top that likely seemed the height of mid-'90s luxury with its smoked glass and city views it is a transient space occupied by a captive market of business travelers and salespeople drinking overpriced, overbrewed coffee.

The general public are not allowed into the festival for the first few days, so an exclusive crowd of publishers, writers, translators and Sweden's innumerable librarians mingle around the hundreds of stalls. Sweden is not even the same size as the Netherlands, yet has a book scene to rival far bigger countries. Each year Stockholm's cultural, political and publishing elite decamp to the west coast to eat canapes, close deals, be seen and market themselves to the world. Gothenburg is more than a book fair; it is a sales event, a political festival and a high point of the social calendar with its mix of writers, celebrities and journalists.

Walking through the exhibition halls is like unfurling a cross section of Swedish society. At one of the stalls a poster of Maria Wetterstrand beams down, promoting her forthcom-ing appearance. Ebba Witt Brattström is there, as are TV chefs, sportspeople and a group campaigning for the release of Dawit Isaak, a Swedish journalist imprisoned indefinitely in Eritrea. It is a seamless mix of culture, hard politics and celebrity. One of the big stories of the 2014 fair is the Swedish rapper Ken Ring, whose autobiography *Life* is about to hit the shelves and make his publisher a significant sum. Ken is the bad boy of the Swedish music scene – he was once arrested for performing a track in which he said he would storm the Royal Palace in Stockholm and make off with one of the royal princesses. His music is a Swedish articulation of American socially aware hip hop, with stories of broken families, racism, lost friends and concrete suburbs. *Life* is being marketed as a brutal and honest insight into his upbringing and his route to localised rap stardom, remarkably dissonant yet perfectly at home in the white middle-class exhibition hall. The previous night Ring performed a set at the fair's opening party in front of Sweden's literati, blonde heads bobbing around the buffet table, sipping on free wine.

Over at the Swedish tabloid *Aftonbladet*'s stand, the feminist comic book writer Liv Strömqvist sits chatting with two journalists in a stylised living room. There are not enough seats for the crowd as they spill out into the adjacent stalls and slump on the floor like an overflowing house party. Strömqvist is known for producing some of the most hilarious, thought provoking and unashamedly laconic graphic work around. Her brilliant book *Prince Charles' Feelings* – based on the Prince's awkward reply to whether he was in love with soon-to-be wife Diana – has been translated into French, but no English publishers have taken the gamble on her unique brand of darkly humorous feminist comics. Her contemporary Lina Neidestam has suffered the same fate – a gifted graphic artist with a killer eye for pseuds and self-analysis, Neidestam remains limited to her home turf.

The reasons Strömqvist and Neidenstam have failed to break out become obvious upstairs in one of the congress hall's conference rooms where the international rights centre lies. A series of tables set up like a speed dating event look out onto the trams humming past in the rain. For 20 minutes at a time Swedish publishers fire names and titles at international reps, all sounding convinced they have the next hit on their hands. At their sides agents and marketing people try and catch the ear of potential buyers and scouts in strange Swedish approximations of LA English more DVD-box-set than Hollywood.

As within its music scene, the Swedish export market is where writers can earn serious money and where the nation can make itself heard. The wave of Swedish crime fiction and thriller translations that began in the 1990s has put the country on the map and made millions for its publishers and agents. People are still pushing crime heavily, with international rights sold on a wave of buzz and hype before the Swedish versions of books have even gone to print. The success of authors such as Stieg Larsson, Henning Mankell and Jens Lapidus has proved highly lucrative, the voyeuristic trips through the dark, fictional underbelly of the Swedish model making for a winning formula with international audiences always ready for new titles. In the film *Blue in the face* Lou Reed said that he found Sweden scarier than New York, and many people would seem to agree.

In addition to the crime wave there is another word on everyone's lips in Gothenburg; feelgood. After the breakout success of novels such as *The Hundred Year Old Man Who Climbed Out The Window And Disappeared* and *The Little Old Lady Who Broke All The Rules*, feelgood has become another banker for shifting Swedish authors overseas. In Swedish the latter book is called *Kaffe med rån*, meaning 'coffee with robbery', and has a subtext dealing with the decline and privatisation of elderly care in Sweden, but the details are of little importance in the broad brush approach of international marketing. Publishers feel good about feelgood's export potential, and naively written stories about the adventures of quirky Scandinavians have struck a chord with overseas markets that can be mined for some time to come.

This emphasis on certain lines of export literature makes it harder for non-genre novels to make the jump into English, and from there into other languages. It is easy to sell a book to a publisher as the new Stieg Larsson, less so as the new Sara Lidman. Crime may be losing its sheen, but it still sells by the truckload to audiences eager for maverick policemen and a touch of the exotic. Downstairs on the shop floor though there is another side of Sweden on show. One whole unit is given over to books solely about old trams and buses in Swedish towns, and another offering homemade travel books boasts a poster of a Scottish bagpiper under a granite sky with the headline 'Scotland, easy to love!'. Over at the stall of a small children's publisher, illustrator Josefin Sundqvist signs copies of her new book, *Pappersväxten*. It will go on to win awards, but there is no media scrum around her table. The hall is dotted with these small publishers, some no more than garage businesses, pushing out books that the big export giants don't deem worth the bother.

Likewise, fan-circles and societies celebrating the work of long-gone greats get their own block. The stall for fans of veteran leftist heavyweight Jan Myrdal – son of Social Democratic icons and Nobel laureates Gunnar and Alva Myrdal – is manned by the legend himself, as if the Berlin Wall were barely cracked. Amongst the crime writers and promotional stands for digital publishing he cuts a lonely, anachronistic figure. There will be few international agents sniffing out his latest novel, written in 1955 and lost in an East German library for half a century. Alongside where he is perched on a collapsible chair the stalls of other past greats with less international currency are guarded by their admirers – Harry

Martinson, Elin Wägner and Stig Dagerman are all kept alive in the corner of the great hall. By the middle of the afternoon everyone has had too much Swedish coffee and the cinnamon buns are running low as people drift toward seminars with spare chairs. At one of them an academic, a translator and a journalist are doing a Q&A on trends. Given the last word, the journalist comes back to the feelgood factor.

Later that night, what seems like half of Gothenburg pack into a nominally ticketed party at a hotel on Avenyn, the city's main boulevard. Ken Ring is there again, standing on the street corner with an entourage. Inside, a successful thriller writer in a very suburban shirt sitting on a Hollywood film deal nervously texts on his phone by the men's toilets, abandoned by his publisher who has gone off to shake hands with someone else. His marketing says he is an international phenomenon, but he could be a travelling businessman booked into the hotel by accident. Being big in Sweden is no guarantee of international success, but Gothenburg is a shop window for a particularly marketable version of the country. If you can talk a good game here then there is a lot of money to be made, but when selling Sweden is about the spreadsheets as much as the reviews, what makes it out is often only a fraction of what stays at home.

* * *

At the opening party for the Gothenburg book fair delegates were met by a dancing man dressed as a bee, shaking to Brazilian techno. The bee belonged to *Expressen*, one of Sweden's biggest newspapers and marketed as 'The Newspaper with Sting'. An integral part of the country's diverse and omnipresent media, *Expressen* have an office in central Stockholm shared with their sister paper. *Dagens Nyheter* and are the main rival to the Social Democratic *Aftonbladet* on the tabloid market. Their political leanings may be different but the headlines in both papers are similar – human interest stories, political revelations and the personal lives of people who are *folkkära*, or loved by the public.

Inside though, Swedish newspapers are remarkably heavyweight. Sweden has never had the same tabloid tradition as Britain or the US – both *Expressen* and *Aftonbladet* have serious political and cultural editorial sections. The presence of both at Gothenburg is not just good marketing but genuine engagement above and beyond sentimental and sensationalist front pages.

Just as elsewhere in the world the print media is in a state of flux. Daily papers are becoming thinner, budgets are being slashed and titles are disappearing as the media moves online and newsprint seems like an indulgence. It used to be a joke in Sweden that everyone was a journalist, but now the opposite is true. Swedish newspapers previously had a global coverage and correspondents filing copy from all continents, but today 24-hour rolling news and the ability to re-write agency reporting has undermined the economics.

Despite this, Sweden has survived the collapse of traditional media better than some similar small nations, in part thanks to the huge annual subsidies which have allowed outlets to manage their transition. At the end of one of Stockholm's metro lines, sitting on the edge of the leafy suburb of Skarpnäck and far from the hip downtown media offices of the city centre, there is a '90s industrial estate of low brick buildings. On the wall of one of them hangs a huge sign reading *Fria Tidningar*, the name of a group of independently run titles that benefit from Sweden's generous system of press support.

The newspaper group is a media cooperative marketing

itself under the banner *'en annan sida av verklighet'*, or 'another side to reality'. Loosely left wing but with a strong green and liberal profile, it was founded at the turn of the last century to provide new perspectives on society, innovative news reporting and a change from the institutitonalised political lines of the country's main titles.

Caspar Behrendt is the man responsible for the direction of *Fria tidningarna*. In charge of editorial development, he sits on the editorial board and works with the editors of the individual titles in the group's portfolio. The offices are divided into neat units running off of a central room, each given over to a team working on one of the more localised editions. For a minority newspaper in a small country the resources available are impressive.

'We have just under 30 full time staff, and then another 20 or so who work part time,' explains Behrendt. In line with global trends, Swedish newspapers increasingly use an army of semi-affiliated freelance staff who work for whoever will pay as and when they are needed.

Without the assistance of the press support model though, *Fria Tidningarnas'* alternative take on politics and society would likely look very different. 'It represents a significant part of our income,' Behrendt says when asked whether or not the paper would work without the support of the taxpayer.

Even with generous subsidies there are parts of Sweden on the way to becoming a media desert. This is already the case in Jokkmokk, a town and municipality high in the Swedish interior, there is no independent newspaper at all reporting on events. 'Jokkmokk municipilaity is as big as Skåne [the region around Malmö] but there is no journalistic monitoring at all,' says Behrendt with concern. 'If something happens people google it and then they end up on Flashback [a popular Swedish web forum] or on sites run by the far right, so it is extremely important that something exists. It does not matter if it is not sensational scandals, just someone ringing round to the police and council to keep tabs on what is happening.'

The press support that keeps many Swedish newspapers ticking over is awarded according to objective criteria. It was started as a way of preventing monopolisation of the media market, making sure that Sweden's towns and cities would have more than one media outlet to provide a plurality of views. Over time its purpose has changed toward underpinning a broader political landscape on a national level. One of the main requirements is that a publication should be able to attract subscribers. Papers such as those published by *Fria Tidningar* appear twice a week and need 1,500 subscribers to qualify. The objective grounds for receiving grants mean that Sweden has a range of minority titles to rival far larger markets, from the left-wing *Flamman* and alternative Stockholm daily ETC through to the newly arrived right wing *Samtiden*, in effect the media arm of the Sweden Democrats which markets itself as 'social-conservative'.

The political diversity of Sweden's media contributes to its healthy climate of debate. *Fria Tidningarna* are owned by their members, so that their leader pages and opinion articles attempt to mirror the general agenda of the membership. In larger media concerns there is a different tack taken, with leader writers chosen by the owners of titles. *Svenska Dagbladet* is a consistent backer of the Moderates, whilst *Dagens Nyheter* has also tended to sympathise with the politics of the Alliance for Sweden of late.

In the new world of click-based journalism though there are fresh challenges to be met. Even with press support, recent fall in revenues has been so great that some titles are little more than shells. Opinion pieces, long an important feature of the Swedish press, have become profitable only if the opinions can draw in web hits, but it is easier to write short news stories than long form reports that cost money to investigate.

'Everyone is a little bit desperate,' admits Behrendt. 'You can't just try and sell advertising, and there is a real reluctance to pay on the web. There's ways to get people to contribute with money but it is just not the same as with a physical newspaper.'

This rapid change creates a headache for the government as much as for the newspapers themselves. Because subsidy is based largely on print distribution figures at all levels, even when media organisations have high web readership they cannot qualify for assistance. In 2016 it is estimated that there will be 68 million kronor in unclaimed subsidy from the pot set aside to support print media. Even for self-defined social-conservatives, change seems inevitable.

* * *

Eight years before George Orwell wrote *1984*, the Swedish Nobel-winning poet Karin Boye produced a lesser known but highly similar science fiction novel, *Kallocain*. Set in a perverted modern state that combined the most extreme elements of European totalitarianism with the rush towards the clinical and futuristic, it described a world in which the state was all and people were mere automatons in an expressionless existence straight from Jan Sjunesson's worst nightmares. Boye's hyper-Stalinist dystopia was located in the early 2000s, a world where technology and efficiency had entirely eradicated the past. It sounded distant enough at the time but *Kallocain* is a work of literary resistance with contemporary relevance, not just against totalitarian thought but for the idea of the self, of free expression and of the ability to articulate basic human compulsions.

The Sweden of the present does not look as Boye feared, but the struggle for expression continues elsewhere on the same continent. Weeks after Bah Kuhnke and the Swedish delegation set foot in Kiev, Ukraine passed laws banning sympathy for the former communist regime and cementing the official role of nationalist militias. The Ukrainian media is dominated by powerful business interests, its Russian counterpart by the state. Creating some kind of free space in between is key to fostering the liberal democracy and cultural diversity of the Swedish media landscape, even if it means spending public money.

After their trip to Kiev, Alice Bah Kuhnke and her team found themselves back in Sweden and in Stockholm's medieval cathedral to bid their final respects to Tomas Tranströmer. Opened up to the general public, there was a long queue to get inside the cavernous building. Members of the Swedish Academy stood behind the wooden pews, and publishers, authors and politicians solemnly said farewell to an icon.

'I don't think any of us can really understand how great he was,' Bah Kuhnke told *Expressen*, the newspaper with sting.

Stepping outside into the chill April silence, the Minister and her team settle on a bench. The next step for the Minister for Culture and Democracy was to be a review of the media subsidy for the digital age, and a manifesto commitment to make sure culture really is available to all. From Kiev to the French Riviera, Gothenburg's exhibition hall and an industrial estate at the end of a subway line, cultural politics is a critical part of Sweden's societal fabric. It may cost, but the country would be a very different place without it.

CHAPTER EIGHT

Metropia

How Sweden built its homes for people

The good home knows no privileged or deprived.

PER ALBIN HANSSON

ON THE OUTSKIRTS of the small city of Uppsala, 40 minutes north of Stockholm is a shallow valley flanked by 1960s tower blocks rising up from behind clusters of pine, their top stories pushing above the treetops. Here in the district of Flogsta the tower blocks make up a gigantic student village, looming above greenery and exposed rock faces in a pattern straight from the drawing board of idealistic midcentury planning. With their inbuilt saunas, air sealed nuclear shelters and collective kitchens they are an anachronistic vision of a cohesive, happy and safe society made concrete.

Across the meadow on the other side of the valley lies the twin suburb of Eriksberg. Whereas Flogsta was intended to provide a home for the eager minds of the next generation, Eriksberg was a new model suburb for working people. Its brick shopping arcades and functional three-storey blocks are replicated across Sweden on the outskirts of countless towns that burst up during the urbanisation, social reforms and economic golden age of the post-war years.

Having been through some tough times, today Eriksberg is finally coming to resemble what its planners first intended. Young families living in three room apartments cycle in and out of the city on segregated paths and take walks in the nearby nature reserve. Green municipal buses running on biogas pull up and disgorge their passengers on a constant loop from the suburb to the city centre and property prices are pushing slowly up as the area gentrifies. One of the newer residents is Patrik Eriksson, a 30-year-old with a young family and a job at the university that dominates the city.

He recently moved up from Stockholm and lives in one of the district's three-room apartments, or *treor* as they known in Swedish. In Sweden the size of flats is given in square metres and the number of rooms – the total minus a bathroom and kitchen – are tallies to mark progression as money allows and family dictates.

'Uppsala is a reasonably big city… but if you're talking about the housing market it is one of the most expensive. Only Stockholm beats it. I think it's more expensive than Gothenburg,' says Eriksson with an air of resignation, 'finding a place was hard, I stayed in Stockholm a year before I was able to get somewhere here. I had a student flat in Huddinge [A suburb in south-western Stockholm], then I was lucky enough to be able to swap it.'

Swaps are an integral part of the ritual of housing in Sweden. If you have a contract on an apartment it is easier to swap with somebody who wants to move into your home than to leave the system entirely. The elaborate bureaucracy that regulates it all is a state within a state.

'When I had to move here I tried to change my apartment in Huddinge. If you have a hire-contract you have the right to occupancy and you can swap with someone else who also has one, it is quite straightforward. Unfortunately nobody wanted to swap with us,' he adds forlornly. 'Sometimes you just have to ring round to people who might have an empty apartment and pester them. That's pretty unfair, otherwise you can get yourself a place in the queue. When I moved to

Stockholm I put myself in the queue after a year or so, and then when I wanted to come here some of the owners in Uppsala had started to advertise their properties through the Stockholm housing queue, so I had eight-years worth of queuing I could use.' Being in the municipal housing queue is the ticket to an assured tenancy, and fixed rent apartments can pass from generation to generation. The highly regulated nature of the system means that some prime locations in the centre of Stockholm are relatively cheap but almost impossible to obtain. Moving to Uppsala or elsewhere is a solution for many people.

'Eriksberg is a nice part of town with a good reputation, even if it was known for being a bit unruly in the past,' Eriksson chimes in optimistically to balance the his frustration at the queue system. 'It is next to some of the poshest areas of villas but is also near to the area that is known for being a bit segregated. I like it there – there is a mixture of hired and owned flats. You meet all sorts of people.'

The neighbouring district with the bad reputation is Gottsunda, a housing project often portrayed as both culturally and geographically separate from the rest of white middle class Uppsala, one of Sweden's oldest cities. Gottsunda regularly features in the local news with stories of burning cars and disenchanted youth. Eriksberg meanwhile has been rebranded as 'New Eriksberg' by developers, with more premium homes on the way to deal with the pressure on the city.

Eriksson lives with his partner and their four-year-old son, their apartment near identical to thousands of others built around the same time. Their building is owned by a private rental company.

'You get everything fixed – if you have a flat with a dishwasher in then the company has to come and fix it. If it wears out they have to change it. The problems is you can't knock anything down,' bemoans Eriksson. 'We have a capped rent that rises a tiny bit each year, but if the market dictated things it would skyrocket. If we had a newer place it would be extortionate too.' New developments command higher premiums, so getting a refurbished '50s or '60s building is often a bargain.

Eriksson's block has a communal laundry room, a common feature in apartments and housing schemes, with industrial washers and dryers. Included in the rent, booking a washing time is a familiar experience to most Swedes. Swedish flats also save space by having their storage elsewhere in the building, with apartments each having a *förråd*, or storage cupboard, in the roof or cellar for everything from skis to unwanted CDs and pans. The entire rent, including fees and utilities, is a little over seven thousand kronor a month, less than half the average wage. Changes to the rent are negotiated through the *hyresgästförening*, a national body representing residents which functions like a union to safeguard the interests of renters. If landlords want to raise rent there is a process that has to be followed, including tribunals. Once inside the system the progression upward begins.

'You can build a kind of housing career,' says Eriksson. 'First you find someone who wants to switch, and then maybe someone else and you can do a triangular switch. I'm pretty happy I've been able to get in. There are other people who have been able to loan money from their parents to buy somewhere, which has made them into millionaires more or less and been able to live more or less. They are essentially living for free as their houses go up in value.'

The two tier system that has developed on the back of a housing shortage in Sweden's cities means that those who can afford to buy can jump the queue system, but the alternative is to deregulate the country's well organised and institutionalised framework that in theory should provide good cheap housing for all. When Marquis Childs visited Sweden in the 1930s there was much which seemed certain to create a bright future that never came to fruition, but what has endured is the organisation of Sweden's housing. Unlike the US and UK, where huge public housing projects were carried out under the direction of the state, even more so the case in Eastern Bloc Europe, Sweden developed housing associations that existed in a place between public and private. Like the welfare aspects of the Swedish model which were developed in lieu of state measures, Sweden's housing was approved and backed by the state but very rarely were the government directly responsible for housing people.

One of the biggest of these organisation was HSB, a cooperative started in the 1920s whose distinctive coat of arms today adorns housing blocks across Sweden. The logic of the coop house was simple, and the earlier designs were often examples of the same Swedish modernism that characterised the aspirational buildings of the Stockholm Exhibition and so inspired Marquis Childs. Childs wrote that:

> Cooperative apartment houses are superior to others in almost every respect, besides being lower in price. They are designed for light, air, convenience and privacy, the new units being in the functional style adopted by younger Swedish architects.

A key part of this were houses grouped into A, B or C classes, mixed together. A was the highest class, B a more modest home and C the cheapest. Most of the costs were met by the authorities even though the homes were managed cooperatively. The result was a rapid growth in cooperative housing, divided into *hyresrätter* where residents paid rent to the housing association and *bostadsrätter* where people purchased the property itself but were still part of a communal organisation.

Rather than physically owning an apartment, owning a *bost-adsrätt* makes you owner of a share of the building with the right to live in an apartment indefinitely. Buildings of both types function in much the same way, but whereas a *bostads-rätt* can be bought and sold on the open market like any other property, getting an apartment for hire often means a long queue.

Another thing that has stayed the same is the constant need for more homes as lifestyles change. In the 1966 local elections Tage Erlander, the veteran Prime Minister who preceded Olof Palme, was asked what a young couple looking for a home in Stockholm should do. His advice was simply that 'they can join the housing queue'. A lack of housing has been a major problem for Sweden's cities over the years, and after the ABC flats of the 1930s a different and altogether more ambitious strategy was taken. Instead of the planned blocks documented by Childs, it was to be a different type of ABC that made the biggest impact on contemporary Sweden. In the postwar years Sweden began to construct large scale ABC suburbs, the letters standing for *Arbete* (work), *Bostad* (housing) and *Centrum* (Centre). Pioneered in Stockholm, the suburb of Vällingby where Olof Palme made his home was a typical articulation of the ABC dream. People would be able to walk from work to home in just a few minutes, all arranged around bustling centres which were modernist reinventions of Swedish small town squares. Vällingby became an inter-national example of the modern Swedish state, attracting global attention and becoming a destination for visiting architects and planners from Western Europe and the US.

The ABC projects were part of a wave of reconstruction in Sweden that tried to break cleanly with the past through its almost total destruction. Central Stockholm was to be rebuilt as a modern functional city, but whereas much of postwar Europe lay in fragments and needed its gaps fillings in, Stockholm was a maze of old streets and wooden houses that had no place in the rational society its architects and politicians envisaged. A plan was developed, called Stockholm 67, which would have involved the demolition of most of Stockholm City Centre and its replacement with huge functional modern office and apartment blocks linked by metro and fast roads. The most extreme aspects of Stockholm 67 never saw the light of day, but it exposed the dissonance between the old picture postcard Sweden and the bright new society that its leaders were trying to create.

These concrete suburbs have become an integral part of public consciousness, transiting from bright future to modern alienation and now slow gentrification. Blackeberg, a newly built area few metro stops from Vällingby, would form the backdrop for John Ajvide Lindqvist's bestselling suburban vampire novel *Let the right one in*. The concrete suburbs that sprang from the ABC project that saw Lindqvist's book become an international hit was a reflection of unintentional urban alienation that resulted from Sweden's well intentioned mass housing projects, in which the threat came not from poverty but from mundane comfort. The theme would be repeated in the films of Roy Andersson, which used the bars and grey walls of the Swedish capital's planned towns as a backdrop for existential reflections on the very experience of being alive. Likewise, Stockholm's crumbling concrete towers were the basis for *Metropia*, a dystopian science fiction adventure by Swedish director Tarek Saleh in which endless housing estates are linked by infinite metro systems and populated by television addicted consumers.

Sweden is not alone in its mixed fortunes with mass housing. The elegant Le Corbusier armchairs on which David Frost interviewed Olof Palme were intended as interior flourishes in functional homes, but the high rises Le Corbusier inspired would become a visual byword for urban segregation across Europe. From Park Hill in Sheffield to Rosengård in Sweden, Lichtenberg in Berlin and suburban Poland, the dreams of a better future for common people have often been undone by the realities of everyday life. Sweden though has emerged from the other side without abandoning social housing entirely, instead reinventing it in new forms more in keeping with the present.

* * *

If you follow the Göta älv River north from Gothenburg city centre the tramline winds its way up the valley into a world of forests and suburban tower blocks. Like in Stockholm, the outer suburbs of Gothenburg are marked by rows of apartments served by transit stops and grouped around small, specially designed squares with generic supermarkets and branches of *Systembolaget*, the government-run alcohol retailer.

Over the valley from the city's first modern suburb, Kortedala, lies the model planned community of Hammarkullen. Outside of Sweden this part of the city is best known as the home of indie troubadour Jens Lekman, who comes from neighbouring Angered. The twee-pop singer songwriter emerged from Gothenburg and onto the international scene in the early 2000s along with a wave of new Swedish indie, writing about growing up in Gothenburg suburbs and riding on its omnipresent trams. Hammarkullen was built as part of the Million Programme, an effort by the Swedish government from 1965 onwards to build a million new homes that people could afford in a phenomenally short period of time. Plans varied, but a large percentage of these new homes consisted of multistory housing blocks in new working-class suburbs like Hammarkullen, complete with its own modern underground tram station and amenities.

In 1997, in response to Sweden falling out of love with its planned communities, the suburb was quite symbolically re-engineered, with one of its largest concrete tower blocks being dismantled piece by piece. One of the advantages of the functional and mass-produced design of the Million homes was that the buildings were in effect just a series of small boxes, the walls of which could be removed and loaded onto flatbed trucks. Just like 'new' Eriksberg in Uppsala, Hammarkullen was to be saved from its own history. In Hammarkullen's case the disassembled apartment blocks were shipped to Eastern Europe to be re-erected, serviceable but sociologically disastrous. Somewhere in Kaliningrad, the Russian enclave on Poland's coastline, there are today low-paid Russians living in the rebuilt shells of Sweden's Social Democratic woodland idylls. The demolition even gave rise to a TV series; *Hammarkullen, or see you in Kaliningrad.* The show portrayed the lives of the people who lived there, from West African immigrants to neo-Nazis, the police and members of the white Swedish working class, all symbolically part of the same huge building.

Sweden's love affair with large scale social suburbs in the social democratic mould is now largely over. Instead it builds new waterside apartments on its post-industrial spaces for people working in post-industrial service jobs. Downriver from Hammarkullen along the Gothenburg shoreline is a very different Eriksberg from the housing project on the outskirts of Uppsala. This Eriksberg is a former shipyard where the dry docks have been converted into pleasant quaysides and the huge looming crane that once lifted sections of ships into place left as a signature landmark for the aspirational district. Painted in bright white across its central beam in block capitals is ERIKSBERG, an unmistakable brand visible from the older rows of apartments across the water. There are no high rises in this Eriksberg, but these are the homes that Sweden now builds. Two or three-stories high, with roof balconies and middle-class amenities, they are model suburbs of a different kind.

If you follow the river further still until it meets the Skaggerak channel and move down Sweden's west coast you arrive in Malmö, another former giant of shipbuilding. Like Eriksberg, Malmö has undergone a waterfront renewal to conceal the wounds left by the removal of its industrial heart. Nowhere is this clearer than in the luxury Turning Torso building which writhes high above the city, gazing out across the Öresund straight to Copenhagen. The signature tower is owned by HSB, a far cry from the simple and functional municipal housing which they pioneered in the 1920s. Rather than being designed according to need, the blueprint was plucked from the pages of an architect's catalogue by an HSB executive who decided that it would be an appropriate marker for his city's reinvigorated waterfront. The whole project cost HSB a significant amount of money, yet after it was built it not everyone wanted to live there. The premium apartments ended up as short term lets, buffeted by the wind across the Öresund and blanched white against the grey mists of the channel.

Despite the changing face of modern Sweden, the switch from social democratic suburbs to executive aspirational apartments has not been a clean break. Ten minutes north of Malmö by train is the city of Lund, its leafy central streets quickly giving way to concrete student housing complexes and small blocks of apartments on the flat landscape. On a clear day the turning torso can be seen rising high above the coastline and the fertile plains of Skåne to the south. Together with Uppsala, Lund's mediaeval university is the closest thing Sweden has to an Oxbridge or Ivy League.

Guy Baeten is an Urban Studies researcher at the university, and has written extensively about the phenomenal changes in Lund, Malmö and elsewhere in Sweden.

'What you see is a continuity between the old Social Democratic housing plans and this new way. You still build huge shopping centres and parking lots and large scale blocks of flats. It is an example of that kind of experiment becoming normalised,' he says. 'There is still an unrivaled belief in the future – what you see is people saying, "we can overcome things just by building".'

The difference now is that those driving the housing market are more often than not developers looking to sell high end developments for profit rather than altruistic politicians. The Öresund region is prime property, offering moneyed residents a quick commute to Copenhagen, high tech jobs in Lund and waterfront Malmö living. 'What is happening now though is that on these large development scales you get superplaces that can be quite far apart but function as one. The Öresund region between Sweden and Denmark is a good example,' Baeten says.

The Western Harbour and its HSB tower are a perfect example of the disintegration of the old fashioned structure of the city. Like a similar redevelopment across Malmö in the suburb of Hyllie, it is ethnically limited in what on paper is Sweden's most ethnically diverse city. In line with the general shift in incomes in Sweden there has been a polarisation in housing, but the system itself is remarkably sound. Walk around a Swedish city and it becomes evident that problems stem from social segregation and inequality, not from the chaotic system of ownership, private letting and low standards that characterise Britain and the US.

'That's where you see a real discontinuity with the past – the social and economic awareness is gone,' says Baeten.

'From the point of view of developers that makes a lot of sense. They just want to build houses and sell them, and the campaign for deregulation of the market as a result. The discrimination is not intentional but is a by-product of the new way of building things rather than any desire to segregate people,' he believes.

There exists legislation in Sweden that demands the provision of housing at a reasonable price, placing the onus on municipalities to build homes their residents can afford. The ongoing housing shortage means that critics of the system have called for more private lets, loosening of rules around rent levels and an even more market-driven housing policy. For now though the system remains more or less intact. Today HSB has 550,000 members, and private landlords are still the exception. The regulated rents mean that tenants have power over their own homes and the very idea of renting has entirely different connotations here than it does across the North Sea – the hardest part is simply finding an available apartment.

The urban Sweden of today is a very different place to the political upheaval and pioneering planning of the 1930s, yet from the clean lines of Gunnar Asplund's modernist homes and the high rises of Hammarkullen through to the white apartments of Eriksberg and the Western Harbour there is one constant; if you have a home in Sweden it will likely be warm, will keep the water out and you will be able to afford it. For many people that would be utopia enough.

CHAPTER NINE

A Moderate Utopia

The new Swedish model

It is a myth that there are no jobs in hard times. There are always positions open.

FREDRIK REINFELDT

'NAZI GOVERNMENT!' shouted Johan Duncanson through the trees of the Slottskogen park in Gothenburg. It was a balmy August day in 2010 and there were only weeks to go until the country was due to go to the polls again after four years of rule by the Alliance for Sweden. The gangly lead singer of the Radio Dept was agitated as he devoted a few seconds between songs to politics, guitar slung in front of him as he faced the crowd at the Way out West music festival.

Fredrik Reinfeldt, the then Prime Minister, had become a fixture in the thoughts of Duncanson and his fellow musicians. The dreampop-infused shoegaze band from Lund achieved modest international fame after they appeared on the soundtrack of Sofia Coppola's *Marie Antoinette*, but on home soil they have a strong line in political songwriting.

When Reinfeldt and his Alliance allies were first elected in 2006, Duncansson penned a song, *Freddie and the Trojan Horse* as a response to the Alliance for Sweden's social reforms. Not content with their first attempt, and faced with a second Alliance term in office, the band followed it up in 2010 with another track, *The New Improved Hyprocisy*. The Trojan horse of the first song's title is a reference to the positive rhetoric that the Moderates and their Alliance partners used to gain power in 2006. The branding project that was unveiled in the Gotland sun became real as Reinfeldt was sworn in as Prime Minister and his number two, Anders Borg, a self-styled modern man and progressive with his earring and ponytail, took over control of the state finances.

Under Reinfeldt and Borg, the 'new workers party', as they styled themselves, pledged to protect and safeguard the Swedish model that it had spent most of its existence arguing against. A central plank of this was one word; *arbetslinjen*, or the work line. Created as a contrast to the *bidragslinjen*, or benefits line, that they claimed the left parties represented, the Alliance told a story in which work was the route to welfare. A benefits society would ultimately undermine the Swedish economy and the generous social provisions that came with it, they argued. It was not a question of helping business, the government had a moral imperative to make it easier to work than not work, it said. The entire rhetorical project of the Moderates and their partners was about the burden of responsibility, not revolution, and the reward for such responsibility came in 2011 when Anders Borg was named Europe's best finance minister by a leading newspaper.

According to the Financial Times, *arbetslinjen* was a Swedish success story that others would do well to follow. The result of the Moderate-led project was a program of fundamental changes to the way the Swedish economic and welfare system was organised, designed to achieve the dream of a streamlined light-blue economy. The fortress of European social democracy was about to fall without ever knowing it had opened the gates.

* * *

Four years after Borg was picked out as Europe's leading economic thinker, it is a bitterly freezing morning in the Stockholm suburb of Skärholmen. The coffee machine is broken at the local newsagents, staffed by a girl switching between Swedish and Kurdish as she serves customers and chats on her hands free mobile. The small shop is located at the entrance to the subway station, constructed in the golden age of social democracy to provide housing for the people as part of the Million programme. The public funicular behind the subway is also broken, and a pensioner contemplates the climb up the long steps to the apartment blocks that sit at the top. From the bench where they are taking a breather they survey the local square, a suburban shopping centre, and beyond it Sweden's largest IKEA warehouse.

At home in the warmth of one of the Million homes, Daniel Suhonen is waiting for his new Swedish sofa to arrive. From the window of his apartment the chimneys and residential blocks of Vällingby, for many years home to Olof Palme, can be glimpsed across Lake Mälaren. The late Prime Minister is commemorated in a photo on the wall of the lounge, surveying the Social Democratic suburbs built on his watch.

Suhonen is more than just a loyal party member though. A political debater, cultural critic for *Expressen*, activist and editor by turns, he has an encyclopedic knowledge of the changes pushed through by Reinfeldt's government. It is a knowledge complemented by a scathing analysis of what the Social Democratic party has become in the face of the changes to the Swedish model. Referred to as one of Sweden's foremost left-wing debaters, he lets out a deep chuckle at the thought.

'There isn't much competition,' he says.

Sweden is littered with people who have come on the same journey as Suhonen, Social Democrats who have fallen out of love with a party that has fallen out of love with social democracy, but few of them make it into the media. At the heart of Suhonen's politics is a concern for the very future of the Swedish economic settlement.

'The Swedish model? There are several levels to it,' he says, 'but the first is really the foundation of a welfare state along Social Democratic lines. When I've written about it we view it as a series of fairly specific solutions used on a wide range of social problems such as unemployment, the collective bargaining systems and trade unions, that need to be strong and the social security system with support from the state. And then there's the tax system. When you look at where we are now after eight years of the last government, and 30 years of what you might call neo-liberal inspired politics, the Swedish model has vanished or been broken.'

The 30 years Suhonen references began, by dark coincidence, just before the assassination of Olof Palme in 1986. As Thomas Piketty so dramatically showed, in 1980 Sweden had the lowest level of inequality in the developed world, but by the early '90s it was beginning to look a lot more like the rest of Europe. Today is it not far behind France. Just like elsewhere in Europe, Sweden seems to be caught in a snowball effect, and having a Social Democratic government once again is not a magic bullet. With this new government we have, if they don't change direction substantially it will be difficult to stop the transition – the process will just roll on a bit like it has done in Britain after Margaret Thatcher. If you do not change course then you can only carry on. And that's probably the most serious issue with this government. The bourgeois parties set in motion a movement which has now become self-reinforcing so that more and more things have come to a tipping point.'

Post-Thatcher Britain functions as a dystopian vision of

the future or something to aspire to depending on where you lie on the Swedish political spectrum. When Centre Party leader Annie Lööf described the Conservative icon as one of her idols, it was perfectly in tune with the Alliance for Sweden project.

'Schools have become so poor and so segregated that people are now starting to have to shield themselves from the consequences of this segregation and the need to protect yourself and counter [the effects of] class-society is creeping downward,' says Suhonen as he sips his coffee. This transformation is not just a question of people choosing parties. Politics is reflexive, and parties make people, he says.

'The great success of the Alliance was setting in motion the market mechanism so powerfully, just as the workers' movement used to be good at creating systems which themselves made people more inclined to have solidarity throughout the 20th century. Now the neo-liberals have made a system which is itself a process,' he reflects. The new generation of young Swedes are Reinfeldt's children. Educated at free schools, encouraged to achieve personal success and alien to the old ways of thinking about society, it is a world in which ethical consumerism and social enterprise have replaced structural change.

'There's a view amongst people on the Swedish left that politics is about being nice,' says Suhonen, 'about showing empathy in one sense, and that is of course good, but these systems shape people above and beyond their ideology. Someone who lives in an area with a good free school and a bad council-run school who chooses the free school isn't evil or neo-liberal... those kind of terms are pretty irrelevant. All that person wants is for their child to go to a good school.'

The free school experiment epitomises Sweden's attempt to introduce choice into a regimented system. In the early '90s a one term coalition government of the non-socialist parties, with the passive support of a flash-in-the-pan populist party called New Democracy, established a system for giving state money to independently run schools, a reform never fully reversed. Upon the Alliance taking power in 2006, free schools became a *cause celebre* for Reinfeldt, who claimed that they would raise standards through competition, specialisation and the liberation of students from the strict confines of a statist curriculum. A word which occurred again and again in the speeches of the Alliance for Sweden was *valfrihet*, or freedom to choose. It meant the freedom to choose a school, to drive or take public transport, to select a healthcare provider and to buy the home you live in. The irony is that, with increasing inequality, choice become a relative concept for many people.

'These mechanisms on society, about what is profitable and what functions for people, they are powerful forces,' says Suhonen pointedly. 'Previously the left had been able to create systems where they could get people to vote for higher taxes on the understanding the system could be relied upon, but now you cannot rely on the system. The new system that the Moderates introduced was about self-reliance and that is an equally powerful framework. You cannot make demands on people to move in any great numbers against society's internal logic. People act according to the logic of the society they are in.'

Within this there is a truth that is hard for many who dream of Swedish utopia to come to terms with – many of the people who voted for the Alliance for Sweden responded to the rhetoric which allowed them to vote for reforms, but also rationally chose to do so and knew very well what was happening.

'I'm against the market but I believe in the market,' says

Suhonen. 'It has an enormous amount of potential – if you pay people to recycle their used bottles it stops them being thrown in the bushes. These market mechanisms are hugely powerful and that is why they need to be regulated because you can see just how much power they have. It often feels like we are in denial about how these mechanisms dictate people's lives. If you can earn money by buying four homes then people will do so.'

Skärholmen is a case in point. Sweden used to have a low bid-rent curve, meaning that property and land prices dropped off substantially outside of city centres. Now though, changes in property prices and a lack of housing in the city means that suburbs further from the centre are even more likely to attract lower earners. In a situation where simply owning a house can be more profitable than working, following the *arbetslinjen* is not a guarantee of freedom.

The statistics on how the Swedish model was changed after 2006 are astounding. To begin with, the government raised the membership fees for trade unions and unemployment insurance. Coming in 2007, it was one of the first points of the reform programme. Previously there had been a flat charge for joining the unions, but variable fees meant that for some people being a union member became six times as expensive overnight and around 130,000 people left the movement altogether according to the estimations of LO. For a person on an average wage the charge tripled, whilst membership fell from over 80 to 68 per cent.

'It was a huge drop off,' says Suhonen, 'and the problem is that the trade unions carry the Swedish model – there's no minimum wage and very little in the way of rights in law. Almost everything is dependent on the union movement. There was a thing with some builders who were working entirely without a bargaining agreement, and that meant they were working 20 metres up in the air on a building site without any kind of insurance. Had they been killed on the job their families back home would not have got a penny, not even to pay for a funeral – it's horrible.'

The situation he describes is not unusual. Cheap labour from the Baltic states is unprotected by the union agreements enjoyed by Swedish workers, and construction companies can also take on cheap workers from the EU without any need to give them the same working conditions. This wage dumping is made easier by low cost transport and the economically precarious nature of the rest of the continent, with European definitions of seasonal workers doing little to help. When Sweden joined the EU in 1994 significant portions of the labour movement were against the decision, whilst the more conservative parties were in favour of opening Sweden up to increased competition and a more fluid labour market.

'Everything depends on the collective agreements in Sweden,' Suhonen makes pains to emphasise. 'They went after the unions so the membership would sink and that weakened their main opponents. The unions were suddenly engaged in a fight for survival.'

The undermining of union movements came in tandem with tax cuts. It used to be the case that the Moderates campaigned purely on tax cuts for the rich, but they changed tack so that everyone working qualified, except for the long term sick and unemployed. This meant that people with jobs in Sweden, many of whom already enjoyed high unionised wages, got even more in their pockets in the short term.

'A lot of people on average wages got a few thousand kronor back in tax rebates, but the people at the top got between 20 and 40 times more back,' says Suhonen with incredulity. The Alliance for Sweden also abolished Sweden's wealth tax, claiming it was unworkable. Those with significant assets and high wages were substantially advantaged, but normal people gained in the immediate term too. There was a perception that the Social Democrats had not been perfect on welfare, and the Moderates were giving them money in their pockets at least. They also abolished the measure of asset accumulation that came with the wealth tax, meaning that it became difficult to tell exactly how much was owned by whom. 'The Moderates are ideologically predisposed towards getting rid of the welfare state but how do you do that without people getting up in arms? You give them a slice of the cake. They channeled more than eighty billion kronor into tax deductions for working people,' he says as he thumbs through a comprehensive list of statistics.

Another plank of the Swedish model that underwent serious change was the health insurance system. By changing the levels of income at which people could claim for health-care, the government sought to move the middle classes towards a market insurance system. This affected higher earners and white collar workers, as a consequence of which they no longer had any need to rely on a public insurance scheme that did not benefit them. These higher earners then got themselves private insurance. Over 70,000 people suddenly found they were uninsured and could not claim any costs. This created an enormous market for private health insurance.

'I think there's several hundred thousand people now with a private healthcare policy in Sweden,' says Suhonen. 'They do it to be sure of care if they fall ill because they cannot rely on the system – it doesn't work.' The actual figure is 570,000, according to industry data.

'They managed to undermine the middle-class welfare model because they knew that these groups had previously had an interest in voting for a more general welfare politics,' he explains, saying that it is typical of the wider practice of removing people from the joined-up welfare system. With no incentive to use common public services, the education system or healthcare, middle and upper classes with assets that can make them money will begin to construct a parallel society.

At the base of Suhonen's misgivings about the direction of Sweden is the same global trend that underpins Thomas Piketty's analysis of the distribution of wealth – once inequality reaches a certain point it will begin to snowball as people secure their private assets. With no incentive to use common public services, the education system or healthcare, middle classes with assets that can make them money will start to construct a parallel society.

Rebranding themselves 'the new workers party' was another masterstroke by Reinfeldt and his PR gurus, the Social Democrats having dropped the same words from the end of their name in public use. Reinfeldt's party claimed to be putting more money in the pockets of the Swedish workforce, but what they gave with one hand they discretely took away with the other. Before 2007 it was possible for people to deduct union membership from their tax returns, just as businesses could deduct the cost of membership to trade associations and lobby groups. This changed the state's neutral position on the Swedish employment market. A bill brought before parliament to change the way the union membership system operated even cited 'irresponsible wage increases which increase unemployment' as the target of the reforms. The aim was to undermine the concept of constantly increasing wages that had underpinned the Swedish model since the Second World War, and the model of employment agreed in the Grand Hotel at Saltsjöbaden 70 years before. After eight years of employment reforms though the jobless rate had actually increased slightly, Sweden had begun to develop a precariat.

Internationally though the new blue of Sweden was portrayed as a reborn middle way, solving the conflict between social welfare and conservatism. The new Swedish model become an inspiration for British Prime Minister David Cameron. Before he was elected to office. Cameron visited Sweden to see how the Moderates had overhauled their toxic image, and he made several trips back before Reinfeldt was shown the door in 2014. Several of the innovations pioneered by Reinfeldt found their way into the British leader's programme for a new modern conservatism. This included tax breaks to employ domestic cleaners and a wave of free schools, as well as an attempt to position the UK as part of a Nordic-Baltic EU bloc forged in the image of the two leaders. The free school experiment was hailed as a revolution in education, but Sweden began to slide down the league tables as reports of money being siphoned off and sub-standard teaching filled the newspapers. In 2015 a report by the Organisation for Economic Cooperation and Development concluded that choice was ruining the Swedish education system and sapping its resources. Even Cameron's concerted effort to prove he was just a normal family man was copied from his Swedish counterpart – Reinfeldt and his ex-wife Filippa, also a Moderate politician, were cast as everyday people from the suburbs, approachable, electable and socially compassionate.

Despite his protestations to be a modern compassionate Conservative, Reinfeldt had a background as one of the staunchest critics of the Swedish model. In 1993 he published a remarkable contribution to Sweden's literary canon, a hybrid work of fiction and political manifesto entitled *Det Sovande Folket*, or *The Sleeping People* in English. It was a dystopian vision of a society of lethargy and decline, drunk on the welfare state and in need of liberation. Most controversially it contained the assertion, 'The Swedes are mentally handicapped and indoctrinated to believe that politicians can create and guarantee welfare.'

The literary merits of Reinfeldt's book were not enough for it to win any of the country's prestigious literary awards, but a theatre company honoured him with a stage adaption in his second term in office. Despite offers of free tickets and public invitations printed in newspapers the Prime Minister never made it to a performance. This aesthetic vision of a Sweden transformed lay at the heart of the project to sculpt a new type of Swedish model. Stig Björn Ljunggren, an expert on the history of Swedish conservatism, noted how, after 2006, Sweden was given a Moderate vision of the everyday. Instead of resisting the future the Reinfeldt project tried to shape it.

The new Moderate Sweden was to be a place full of happy, healthy and hardworking people enjoying the fruits of their own labour. Even when they are not in power, modern Stockholm is a Moderate city with its Volvo-ready road tunnels, increasingly expensive inner suburbs and obvious lifestyle politics. Bright and clean and green and healthy, and very wealthy, it has some of the highest quality of life in Europe for those who can afford it.

It is also easy to see the link between the Trojan horse politics of the Swedish Moderates and the explosion of the far right in their eight years at the helm. Having spent two terms opposing the Alliance for Sweden, in 2014 the Radio Dept released a third song – *Death to fascism*. This time it was addressed to the far-right insurgency. Disenfranchised and nostalgic for the security of the past, it is easy to see why the easy solutions promised by the Sweden Democrats are a siren sound for many.

Sweden after Reinfeldt is not exceptional – it looks remarkably similar to many countries across Europe struggling with the consequences of globalisation and political fragmentation. However, after eight years of the streamlined, modernised Swedish model, the real question remains unanswered; has the freedom people were given made them happier? Olof Palme said that we are doomed to live on this earth and should make life as agreeable as possible. Reinfeldt meanwhile wanted to set Sweden free, but his ideal new Swedes failed to emerge from their shells.

In Skärholmen the windowless budget supermarket built into the concrete of the hillside advertises cut-price bargains and the modernist church punts its lunchtime soup deals for the lonely. The shopping centre opposite, meanwhile, shields the square, devoid of people, from the roar of the motorway and the cars funneling into the IKEA car park. The Trojan horse may be gone, but it has left an empty space at the heart of Social Democracy's fortress waiting for something to fill it.

CHAPTER 10

A Utopia Like Any Other

How Sweden's future is everyone's future

> Accept the present reality – only then can we
> master it.

GUNNAR ASPLUND

THE SKYSCRAPERS AND new-build suburbs of Shanghai that have pushed the price of Swedish iron ore up and dragged it down again sprawl under a hazy spring sky. Container ships roll past the mouth of the Yangtze River on their way out into the world through the East China Sea, packed with mass-produced Chinese exports. A few miles inland from the riverbank sits a container factory, welding together the metal boxes that carry Chinese goods to Western markets. Some of them will likely end up stacked on the quayside in Gothenburg, unloading from Maersk container ships for Scandinavian consumers.

Thousands of miles from the North Sea, Sweden is nearer than you might think to the Chinese metropolis. Next to the container factory kicking out boxes to hold the world's consumer products sits an awkwardly placed model suburb, designed to accurately represent small town Sweden in almost every way. Its neat shopping streets are borrowed from Stockholm's earlier garden dormitory towns and conform to the same rules of spacing as the new Kiruna, and the same colours as Vimmerby's fantasy high street. On the edge of Swedish Town meanwhile lies the Lake Mälaren Golf Club, a luxury course that has hosted some of the world's top pro golfers, with aspirations to be a forest fringe of Stockholm rather than the mud flats of Shanghai.

Swedish Town's transplanted homes lie in a district called Baoshan, at the tip of Shanghai's giant transit network. In the last ten years the Chinese city has built more subway lines than Sweden did in the entire 20th century. The area is minutes away from the terminus of Line 7 – the vaguely approximated Meilan Lake – one of the busiest on the exploding Shanghai metro system that struggles to keep up with the ever more distant city rim. Opened in 2009, it sits on a concrete viaduct above an urban motorway, linking together the sprawl of interconnected suburbs that make up Shanghai's Pudong district. Pudong was once an area of Chinese farms and factories across the water from the various European owned concessions of the Belle Epoque that made small numbers of people very rich. Nowadays it is a conurbation housing Shanghai and China's new urbanites. The line itself doesn't stop at anywhere of particular import, but like the winding tram and metro lines of Gothenburg and Stockholm it binds the city together under one nominal banner.

At the centre of Swedish Town lies the oblong Meilan Lake itself, a few minutes' walk from the station and visible from the concrete metro viaduct. The supposed centerpiece of this little piece of Scandinavia, on its edge sits a four star hotel and conference centre that finds use with couples taking their wedding photos, as well as local mums strolling with their babies in long circuits around its perimeter. The marketing information for Swedish Town boasts about a supposed replica of (Danish) Copenhagen's famous Little Mermaid in the lake, but it is invisible if it does exist.

The entire complex was built by a firm of Swedish architects as part of one of China's centrally mandated five-year plans. In a ring around metropolitan Shanghai, planned communities sprang up that aped parts of the world far from China, signaling progress beyond the identical tower blocks of the country's economic boom. They were supposed to be modern and aspirational, whilst at the same time existing in an imagined Europe that had never been real. Alongside the more prosaic Swedish looking buildings there also sprang up ornate Alpine palaces from Germanic fairytales and what claims to be a replica of the Icelandic parliament.

In this miniature Scandinavia robbed of its context there are still similarities to the real Sweden. Wealthy middle-class families buy up the properties knowing that they will increase in value and can be sold on. Audis and 4x4s park up outside blocks of urban apartments like in the pricier parts of Stockholm, and public sculpture showing naked European bodies decorates street corners. Sweco, the multinational firm behind Swedish Town, specialises in 'sustainable architecture', but the haphazard and often polluted world of Shanghai has crept slowly into their creation. Before the arrival of this transplanted piece of Sweden, Meilan Lake used to be a shopping outlet, selling discount, off-season clothing. Today business is not great, with only one sportswear outlet left. Most of the shops are now vacant, but there is still a children's playroom. It is just that though – there is no *förskola* in Swedish Town for Baoshan's children to play at in the open air.

The main stretch from Meilan Lake station to the Lake Mälaren golf club is the heart of this miniature recreation of Sweden, and it is here that the most explicit replicas of Scandinavian architecture and cityscapes pop up. They are built as retail properties even though they look like cottages, gambling on shoppers being attracted to the idyllic Nordic shopping streets and European-style marketplaces.

From its idyllic outline, Swedish Town is changing as the planned model around which it was based falls victim to the external pressures of Chinese markets and Chinese capitalism, and by extension the wider world. Immediately outside the

metro station is a small modern mixed-use commercial comp-
ound of Soho loft style apartments. Many of them stand
empty and some are being renovated to sell on. They are
little more than bare shells, a concrete box with only basic
drainage and cabling so that buyers can do what they like
without having to worry about the constraints of the Scandinavian template.

Further away from this hollowed out shell of Sweden
there are newer homes with different values. Dwarfing the
Nordic houses are English-style gated communities, but their
palatial sales office lies abandoned, joined by an identical
project directly behind the retail park by the lake. Though
the area is officially known as Swedish Town (confirmed by
a curious local), the prime residential compounds now advertise themselves as the embodiment of a British lifestyle, one
of trim gardens, townhouses and social exclusivity infinitely
more marketable to moneyed Chinese. Pressing further east,
deeper into the planned heart of Swedish Town, there is an
enormous Disney-like castle which houses a major maternity
hospital. The roads and greenery become less immaculate the
further you move across the fading Scandinavian outpost as
it begins to look more and more like any other Shanghai
suburb. Increasingly this little indulgence of Nordic fantasy
architecture really only exists in name, and in time it may be
reduced to nothing more than an historical curiosity. Cut off
from its natural surroundings, Swedish Town seems almost
inevitable that it should fade out into Chinese modernity.

The real Sweden is, for the time being at least, more
actively resisting the world around it than its Chinese counterpart. The phenomenal Chinese economy that pays for model
Swedish towns and model English gated communities has
averaged almost ten per cent growth year on year for the past
30 years. Like most of Western Europe, Sweden has had a

somewhat less impressive increase in its wealth, and if Thomas Piketty is right then the days of exponential growth are not set to return, however many reforms and budget cuts European governments institute.

One of the arguments of the Alliance project that transformed Sweden was that structural reforms to the Swedish economy would push growth and help to preserve welfare in the new globalised marketplace the country found itself in. After he was removed from government by Sweden's unhappy voters, former Finance Minister Anders Borg authored a remarkable comment piece for the World Economic Forum in which he talked about the need to 'front load' economic reforms, getting them passed in the early days of a government just as his party had done in 2007. He then expressed surprise that Swedish growth rates had dropped – the whole package had been built on the idea that economic growth would follow market reforms in much the same way it had been seen to previously.

Then the global economic crisis hit and an election arrived which Borg claimed was largely about the integration of immigrants, with the 'real' issues being ignored by the electorate. He also argued that statistics were in his favour – those who voted for reform were 'better educated' and asset rich. In a broad brush approach, those who did not vote Moderate were dismissed as standing in the way of progress. What never crossed Borg's mind was that people were actively resisting something far larger, whether they voted red, green, pink, or even brown.

Contemporary Sweden, in its experience of upheaval and fragmentation, is remarkably similar to the rest of Europe, with large old Social Democratic parties trying to keep themselves relevant but unable to offer much beyond slightly less painful reform packages that aim to increase growth. In

Sweden the basic rules of the economy are no different than in Britain or France, Germany or the US, China or Ireland.

When Thomas Piketty appeared on *Skavlan* to pull apart Bjørn Kjos' claims of poverty he added a dose of substance to the otherwise superficial world of the prime time chat show. His argument was that Sweden had previously been as unequal as the rest of the world during the early years of the 20th century, and that it took two world wars and half a century of consistent political choices to mitigate that. Piketty himself told the Stockholm studio audience 'I do not believe in determinism... it is about the policies we make.' Sweden has historically been immensely successful in policy choices, coming up with solutions to meet the specific challenges of the modern world whilst trying to build a better one. Contrary to the essentialist idea of the country as a society of innately virtuous and hardworking egalitarians, as Marquis Childs so eagerly reported to his foreign audience, it was not born equal but picked a path through the changing present. Sweden managed to deviate from the international norm for a large part of the 20th century before moving slowly back, and the direction it now takes is, like anywhere else, a question of choice. The TV studios where Piketty sat down opposite Fredrik Skavlan on comfy leather chairs were the same ones where David Frost and Olof Palme met almost half a century earlier to discuss the success of the Swedish model and the country's modern project. In 1969 the world looked to Sweden and Sweden duly obliged, but in the intervening years no other country outside of Scandinavia ever came close to replicating what Sweden achieved in the postwar era. For all the admiration, it was Anglo-American capitalism that won out.

China's fading Swedish town is a concrete example of how copying the Scandinavian dream is often only a superficial exercise, from the free schools of the British Conservative party to the overtures of Scottish Nationalists and the signature Nordic buildings that have popped up around the world as physical statements of something nebulously modern and progressive. There is a danger that in this enthusiasm for all things Swedish its imitators build something as real as the caricatured high street of Vimmerby with its sweet shops and wooden houses behind their high wire fence. Like the Chinese shoppers in Meilan Lake buying their discount sportswear, it is easy to be sold the Swedish model without really knowing what it is.

For those who continue to look enviously north in search of inspiration and might be tempted by their own Swedish model villages, the question is which particular Sweden they wish to imitate. The nostalgia for the postwar welfare settlement in Britain and the US which has strengthened in the face of increasingly brutal government spending plans and political upheaval would not find much to relate to in the Sweden of today, a place where the appetite for large scale social engineering is non-existent and the idea of using central government funds to run the welfare system an unpopular concept. For most of its life the Swedish system existed between two worlds, firstly between Anglo-Saxon capitalism and European totalitarianism and latterly between post-war Western capitalism and the Eastern Bloc, meaning its development cannot truly be understood in the terms of either.

Both financially and culturally, the world in 2016 is a much more complex place than it was in 1930, with the increase in the liquid flow of capital and the consequent accumulation of assets playing out on a global scale previously unseen. As Piketty points out, contemporary Sweden does not look entirely different from many other Western economies in terms of its general direction but the caveat for Sweden is that it mitigates certain aspects of the usual pattern of social stratification through specific social policies, trade union strength, its emphasis on gender equality and an attitude to public goods that is not present elsewhere.

For the voters of Scotland who had been promised a Nordic-style state by the Scottish National Party things would inevitably have ended in disappointment. The most important plank of the Swedish system, a strong trade union movement and a move towards higher wages, was almost entirely absent from Scotland's blueprint for the future. Most political parties in Britain are committed to a legislated minimum wage. This would be largely incompatible with the Swedish system of labour relations, and a move toward the Swedish system would undermine the so-called Beveridge model of welfare in which the state acts as guarantor and agent on almost all aspects of redistributive policy. As the past and current UK governments show, however, such heavy state involvement also leaves the welfare system open to attack by giving it almost total control. For Britain to pursue a Swedish labour model it would need the trade union movement to double its membership and completely rethink its entire approach to industrial relations. At a time when a rhetorical preoccupation with market choice prevents British politicians from establishing new comprehensive public institutions, Sweden still possesses a number of important communal services, from publicly run transport to its public nursery and higher education systems, all used by large numbers of people. Although it has marketised their delivery in some areas, it has not attempted to abolish or selectively implement them as the UK has done. If Britain were to copy Sweden it would need to make its education system totally free at the point of use once again, abandon its deregulation of large tracts of public transport, tackle the embedded inequalities of a divided private and public education system, develop a mechanism to stop spiraling housing costs and roll out public nursery care. All this would merely be a first step towards a baseline imitation of the most visible features of the Swedish social settlement.

None of these measures have come up for serious consideration by any of the major political parties in the UK or North America. Where conflicts between public goods and private interest have arisen, Britain and the US have repeatedly failed to safeguard their common assets. This is not to say that Sweden is infallible, but rather that Britain and many another developed countries have utterly failed to grasp and protect the value of their shared spaces and institutions.

An important component of this approach is the politics of tax and spend, where rather than tax being used merely as a redistributive measure it is ploughed into common good services. The OECD estimates that Sweden's total revenue and spending is more than 50 per cent of its total GDP. Even under the nominally left-wing government of Tony Blair, the UK still had a lower level of public expenditure than Sweden under its eight years of right-wing Alliance government. With an increased aversion to public spending and an apparent ideological dislike of welfare as a general principle, Britain is currently moving even further away from any semblance of a Nordic settlement.

In the everyday crises faced by many people in Britain, an approximation of the Swedish model would undoubtedly lead to an improvement in their lives, not least in terms of higher wages to reduce income disparity and lift people into the tax system. In its time in power the British Labour party used a programme of tax credits to subsidise low pay in the UK, whilst the Conservatives and Liberal Democrats chose to raise the income tax threshold instead of tackling the root cause of low wages. Likewise London, the most extreme articulation of the hyper-capitalist city in Europe, would be a very different place if it had capped rents and Sweden's cooperative housing schemes.

The English capital is also a good example of the limitations of the old Swedish model in the modern world, with its tendency towards geographical and personal concentration of wealth. Piketty's analysis of the global economy stretches far beyond an interest in the curious outlier that was Sweden in the early 1980s. Although it may have managed the changing situation in different ways on home soil, the same macrotrends in inequality have apparently emerged regardless. That much-admired Swedish model, which grew as a largely national response to economic circumstance within a 20th century nation state, is only one component in a global picture that is perpetually changing.

Like any country, Sweden is limited and guided by the context in which it finds itself, from mineral trading to the Chinese consumer goods market and the affordability of the Thai tourist industry to its holidaymakers. The choices about the future which Thomas Piketty stressed in his Swedish television appearance were related to the recognition of circumstance and need as much as utopianism. One of those suggested choices would be the institution of a tax on financial capital to both alleviate inequality and pay for investments in what economists refer to as natural and human capital – fighting climate change, preserving common institutions and dealing with global problems in a worldwide social-democratic consensus.

Where the Swedish model and its domestic achievements are now headed is uncertain. Where change is afoot in Sweden, it is through the fragmentation of politics and the emergence of new voices, through new parties seeking on the one hand to pull the centre towards a greener, more feminist future and on the other to retreat to an imagined secure and ethnically homogenous past. The only certainty in all of this is that, more than ever before, Sweden's problems are the world's problems and the world's problems are Sweden's problems. The big issues of the age, human rights, inequality and the environment, are global, replicated from Stockholm to Scotland and beyond. In different forms, the dilemmas of contemporary Sweden are mirrored across Europe, and Europe's problems are mirrored across the world.

Gunnar Asplund's call in the book written to accompany the Stockholm Exhibition of 1930, *Acceptera*, was to 'accept the present reality – only then can we master it'. It was a call to work towards a future that met the needs and challenges of the present, one built on the choices society collectively makes. It meant understanding that the world was changing and rising to meet it, because as Sweden has found, history is never over even if you are ahead of the pack.

On the same spot where Asplund's shining restaurant marked 'Paradise' and the other exhibits that so inspired Marquis Childs once stood, there today sits the Swedish Technical Museum. Greeting visitors as they enter the museum is a particular kind of Swedish model, one in which miniature trains in orange and brown snake through a picturebook landscape of hills and forests. Children stand on tiptoes as the tiny coaches and bright locomotives with electric flashes run in circles in a perfect recreation of a late 1940s idyll. Under their feet is a model of the Kiruna iron mine, down the hallway in one direction a display on the digital revolution, and in the other a collection with the subtitle 'back to the future'. For over half a century this particular Swedish model has sat surrounded by the techno-utopian dreams of days to come, and Sweden is and always has been a utopia like any other. It is in that malleable future that all utopias are made.

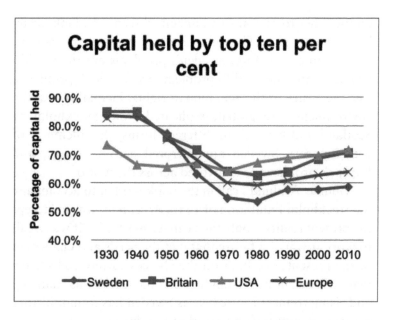

Reproduced from http://piketty.pse.ens.fr/files/capital21c/en/
pdf/supp/TS10.1.pdf – Concentration of wealth in Europe and
in the USA, 1810–2010

Unless stated otherwise all statistics on national economy
and employment are from Statistics Sweden (SCB). The
relative value of Swedish currency in articles is based on
exchange rates in July 2015.

Recommended reading

Etzemuller, T. *Alva and Gunnar Myrdal: Social Engineering in the Modern World*. Lexington books; New York; 2014

Hilson, M. *The Nordic Model: Scandinavia since 1945*. Reaktion Books; London; 2008

Pred, A. *Even in Sweden*: Racisms, Racialized Spaces, and the Popular Geographical Imagination. University of California Press; Berkley; 2000

Bauman, Z. *Liquid Modernity*. Polity Press; London; 2000

Piketty, T *Capital in the 21st century*. Belknap Press; Cambridge MA; 2014

Wollstonecraft, M. *Letters written during a short residence in Sweden, Norway and Denmark*. Oxford University Press; Oxford; 2009

Childs, M. *Sweden: The Middle Way*. Yale University Press; Newhaven; 1947

Brandal, N & Bratberg, O. *The Nordic Model of Social Democracy*. Palgrave Macmillan; London; 2013

Eckersley, R: *The Green State: Rethinking Democracy and Sovereignty*. MIT Press; Cambridge MA; 2004

Luath Press Limited
committed to publishing well written books worth reading

LUATH PRESS takes its name from Robert Burns, whose little collie Luath (*Gael.,* swift or nimble) tripped up Jean Armour at a wedding and gave him the chance to speak to the woman who was to be his wife and the abiding love of his life. Burns called one of 'The Twa Dogs' Luath after Cuchullin's hunting dog in Ossian's *Fingal*. Luath Press was established in 1981 in the heart of Burns country, and now a few steps up the road from Burns' first lodgings, Edinburgh's Royal Mile. Luath offers you distinctive writing with a hint of unexpected pleasures.

Most bookshops in the UK, the US, Canada, Australia, New Zealand and parts of Europe either carry our books in stock or can order them for you. To order direct from us, please send a £sterling cheque, postal order, international money order or your credit card details (number, cardholder and expiry date) to us at the address below: post and packing as follows: UK – £1.00 per delivery seas surface mail – £2.50 per delivery address; overseas £3.50 for the first book to each delivery address, plus additional book by airmail to the same address. If your order happily enclose your card or message at no extra charge.

Luath Press Limited
543/2 Castlehill
The Royal Mile
Edinburgh EH1 2ND
Scotland

Telephone: 0131 225 4326 (24 hours)
email: sales@luath.co.uk
Website: www.luath.co.uk